T0354457

Stories from The Law of Attraction

The Good, the Bad and the Funny

Judi Mason
And Many Co-Creators

BALBOA.
PRESS
A DIVISION OF HAY HOUSE

Balboa Press books may be ordered through
booksellers or by contacting:

Balboa Press
A Division of Hay House
1663 Liberty Drive
Bloomington, IN 47403
www.balboapress.com
1 (877) 407-4847

Because of the dynamic nature of the Internet, any web
addresses or links contained in this book may have changed
since publication and may no longer be valid. The views
expressed in this work are solely those of the author and do
not necessarily reflect the views of the publisher, and the
publisher hereby disclaims any responsibility for them.

The author of this book does not dispense medical advice or
prescribe the use of any technique as a form of treatment for
physical, emotional, or medical problems without the advice of a
physician, either directly or indirectly. The intent of the author is only
to offer information of a general nature to help you in your quest for
emotional and spiritual well-being. In the event you use any of the
information in this book for yourself, which is your constitutional right,
the author and the publisher assume no responsibility for your actions.

Any people depicted in stock imagery provided by Getty Images are
models, and such images are being used for illustrative purposes only.
Certain stock imagery © Getty Images.

Print information available on the last page.

ISBN: 978-1-5043-9912-8 (sc)
ISBN: 978-1-5043-9914-2 (hc)
ISBN: 978-1-5043-9913-5 (e)

Library of Congress Control Number: 2018902484

Balboa Press rev. date: 04/18/2018

Contents

Part 3 The Funny

Part 4 Children's Stories

Part 5 Inspired Actions

For Greg, Christine, Rebecca,
Joshua, and Denielle:
You are my light, my love, and my inspiration.

Preface

I love listening to stories, I love reading stories, and I love telling stories. Stories have a way of teaching us effortlessly, often in a way where our left brain logic gets out of the way and stops interrupting because they are just stories (aren't they?). Stories can make us laugh, and they can make us cry; they can make us think about our own stories, and they can, and often do, inspire us. So when I received the inspiration for this book, I was elated.

I was sitting in the car one morning listening to *The Law of Attraction* on compact disc. I had been going through some very challenging months, and I was enjoying listening to the CDs again, so I was just in the zone. Suddenly, the idea for this book just popped into my head. Although I had written several short stories, I hadn't seriously thought of writing a book before. The idea resonated with me because I had often told stories about manifesting, and I knew that many people connected with the stories and also enjoyed sharing their own stories. I was so excited about it, and it changed my whole perspective instantly. Previously, I'd had an urge to write down everything that had gone wrong for me over the past couple of months, and I had resisted that urge because I knew about the law of attraction. I was trying to focus on positives. However, it was always there in the background and was affecting how I was feeling.

After I received the inspiration for this book, the urge returned, so I sat down and listed everything that had gone wrong over the past three months. After I finished that, I wrote down everything that had gone right in the same time frame. I ended up with about one page of negatives and three pages of positives, and I felt great. I had purged the negatives and was able to completely focus on, and be grateful for, all of the positives in my life. One of those positives was the idea for this book. I hadn't been this excited about something for a long time. I started talking to people about their stories, and amazing things began to happen. Everyone was getting excited about this book, and they now remembered things in their lives where they had created what they wanted (and sometimes what they didn't want), so everyone was now focusing on the law of attraction.

One friend said to me, "Thank you for doing this because while I'm thinking about the stories for you, I'm in the zone and attracting more positive things to me, so I just keep manifesting more stories for your book." So before this book was even written, it was already having a positive impact on many people.

I hope you also enjoy the stories and feel both inspired and empowered.

Acknowledgements

I would like to thank all of the contributors to this book; I honour you all for your enthusiasm and willingness to share your personal stories, which have added so much joy and inspiration.

I would like to express my great appreciation to Jackie Shanks for her help in editing and her continued encouragement throughout the final stages of this book.

To all of the great teachers and my mentors, from whom I have learnt so much, I am forever grateful.

To my wonderful husband, Greg, for all of your support, encouragement, and hours of patiently listening to my stories.

To my children, who have all contributed to this book, Christine, Rebecca, Joshua, and Denielle, their partners, and my seven grandchildren. You are all a constant source of inspiration and pride.

To Dad (in heaven) and Mum and to all of my wonderful family and friends who have enriched my life, just by being there. Thank you.

Introduction

I am always amazed every day by the many and varied ways the law of attraction works, from random phone calls or books falling off the shelf to your feet to unusual hunches to go somewhere or look at something to simply thinking about someone, and then a few seconds later, getting a call from them. These synchronicities are all around us. The more we become aware of it, the more we see it happening, and it adds some magic to our lives.

I find it very empowering to know that we can create what we want, and I am so grateful to be living in the awareness of what I am feeling and therefore manifesting.

Along with many of my own stories, people of all ages and from all walks of life have contributed stories to this book. Some of the stories are very short, and some quite long, but they are all true stories told by each person in their own, unique way about their personal experiences.

The book is divided into five parts: "The Good," "The Bad," "The Funny," "Children's Stories," and "Inspired Actions."

"The Good" is the largest section of the book. It's filled with a variety of stories about things, people, health, wealth, and events that have been created by deliberately using the law of attraction, consciously focusing on what was wanted, and, even more importantly, being open to receive it: from little things such as a bunch of flowers to something grand like a diamond. Some things seem easier to manifest, but that is only because we believe that it's easier. For example, a bunch of flowers would be nice, but there is very little importance put on it; it doesn't really matter whether we have it or not, but it's a nice thought. In this scenario, there is no resistance to receiving the flowers. However, in the case of money, for example, we might really need that, and therefore, we put much more importance on the outcome of that manifestation; this puts us in a different vibration, and it seems harder to manifest. If we could take the same approach (light-hearted, easy-going) as we did with the flowers, we could manifest whatever we desire.

In the next section, "The Bad," I have included a selection of stories whose aim is not to focus on bad things happening, but to show how we need to be more aware of what we consciously and unconsciously ask for. Since my husband, Greg, and I have been learning about the law of attraction, we occasionally notice each other blurting out something (old habits) that we do not want to create in our lives, so we often remind each other to be more conscious. Many times, it is so ingrained in our habits, we are not even aware we are saying it. Things such as "He's a pain in the neck," or "I'd die for [whatever] right now," "I nearly had a heart attack," "That drives me crazy," and so on. Once we become aware, it's quite surprising how many of these old sayings we blurt out.

This section is to make us realise that we are creating all the time and once we become aware of that, we can change our old habits and consciously ask for what we really do want to create in our lives. I had a difficult time collecting stories for this part. It is the smallest section of the book. I think that is because, in hindsight, something that seemed "bad" at the time actually ended up being "good," and as you'll see, although I have placed some of these stories in the bad section, they really do have positive outcomes.

The stories in "The Funny" section are examples of remembering to be specific when we ask for something. There are many stories here of how the law of attraction gives us *exactly* what is asked for, even if that was not what we really meant. For example, I met a lovely lady who was telling me she always used to say, "I want to marry a rich man." The name of the man she married was Ritchie, and everyone called him Rich, so she did, in fact, marry a rich man; he just had very little money.

Then there is the "Children's Stories" section. Children are true creators. They are born knowing much more than we give them credit for but are often told that they can't have everything they want. It was in childhood that most of us learnt about phrases such as "Money doesn't grow on trees" or "Money is the root of all evil." Well, you get the idea, but now with more awareness of the law of attraction, the younger generation is growing up with much less resistance and fewer negative belief patterns to overcome.

Finally, there is a section on "Inspired Actions" of the law of attraction, such as creating vision boards, meditation, visualisation, and much more to get you focusing in the direction you want to go.

It's nice to be reminded that the law of attraction is happening all of the time, and we are the only ones who block it, so as you read these stories, I hope you laugh. I hope you smile. I hope you are as inspired as I have been, and may you remember your own stories and your own power to create whatever it is that you want in your life.

What Is the Law of Attraction?
How Does It Work?

"The Law of Attraction says: 'That which is like unto itself is drawn,' which means vibrations are always matched. So as you experience the contrast which inspires the new idea within you, this new idea—this desire—whether it is a strong one or a soft one, is summoning unto itself proportionately. And as it summons, it is always answered. It is the basis of our universe: When it is asked, it is always given. The confusion that humans feel is that they think they are asking with their words—or even with their actions—and sometimes you are. But the universe is not responding to your words or your action. The universe is responding to your vibrational calling."

—Abraham

[1] Excerpted from the workshop in Cincinnati, Ohio, on Saturday, July 15, 2000.

The law of attraction is a law, just like the law of gravity. It's working, whether you believe it or not.

I have been consciously learning about the law of attraction over the past thirty years; I have had many teachers, read many books, been to workshops, and discussed it in groups and with friends. Of course, unconsciously, I have been learning about this my whole life; sometimes, the lessons have been hard ones, which is why it is better to understand the law and become conscious creators rather than unconscious or accidental creators.

When I was a very young child, I had some profound experiences, and one of them I remember vividly. It involved the law of attraction and the law of gravity together. I was only about six years old, and I was playing near an old quarry with a friend. I wasn't supposed to be playing there because my parents considered it too dangerous. I was dancing and jumping and playing around at the top of a deep ravine, and I fell. At that moment, time slowed down, and everything seemed to go in slow motion. I prayed to God to save me. I then felt hands around my waist, and I was being spun around and gently placed down on my feet at the bottom of the ravine.

I immediately looked up at my friend, who was still standing at the top. She asked, with a very shocked look on her face, "How did you do that?"

I asked, "Do what?"

She replied, "Do a somersault in mid-air and land on your feet."

I didn't tell anyone about that incident because I was afraid I'd be in trouble for being in the quarry, and in any case, children just accept things like that. It wasn't until I was much older that I realised how unusual and extraordinary that incident was. It was an example of the law of attraction because I asked, and I was open to receive. As a child, it seemed to come unconsciously; there was no resistance. There was always the expectancy that I would be answered, and it seemed like I always was. It was only when I grew older that I started to question why. Thus began my quest to understand the law of attraction, even though I had no name for it at the time.

This book has nothing to do with anyone's religion or their personal beliefs; whatever sits right with you is right for you.

We can say God, the angels, the universe, spirit, source, and more. We can talk about prayer, meditation, visualisation, or anything else, but everything is energy; therefore, when we ask, pray, meditate, or visualise, we are changing our vibration/energy to attract or create that which we are asking for. How we feel about anything is more important than what we say or what names we use.

Good, Bad; Who Knows?

There once was a farmer. One day, the farmer's only horse ran away. The farmer's neighbours, all hearing of the horse running away, came to the farmer's house and all said, "What bad luck!"

The farmer replied, "Maybe it is; maybe it isn't."

About a week later, the horse returned, bringing with it a whole herd of wild horses. The neighbours, hearing of the horses, came to see for themselves. As they stood there looking at the horses, the neighbours said, "What good luck!"

The farmer replied, "Maybe it is; maybe it isn't."

A couple of weeks later, the farmer's son's leg was badly broken when he was thrown from one of the wild horses he was trying to break. The neighbours, all hearing of the incident, came to see the son. As they stood there, the neighbours said, "What bad luck!"

The farmer replied, "Maybe it is; maybe it isn't."

At that same time, there was a war going on. In need of more soldiers, the army sent one of their captains to the village to conscript young men to fight in the war. When the captain came to take the farmer's son, he found a young man with a broken leg. Knowing there was no way the son could fight, the captain left him there. The neighbours, hearing of the son not being taken to fight in the war, all came to see him. As they stood there, each one said, "What good luck!"

The farmer replied, "Maybe it is; maybe it isn't. Who knows?"

—Tao Parable

Part 1

The Good

"Love and appreciation are identical vibrations. Appreciation is the vibration of alignment with who-you-are. Appreciation is the absence of everything that feels bad and the presence of everything that feels good.
"When you focus upon what you want, when you tell the story of how you want your life to be, you will come closer and closer to the vicinity of appreciation, and when you reach it, it will pull you toward all things that you consider to be good in a very powerful way."

[2] Extract from *Money and the Law of Attraction: Learning to Attract Health, Wealth, and Happiness.* By Jerry Hicks and Esther Hicks. The Teachings of Abraham

"You create your own universe as you go along."
—*Winston Churchill*

A Perfect Day (One of Many)

I had quite a lot to accomplish on this particular day, and I was already in the car, ready to go shopping, when I got the urge to meditate first. So I listened to my inner voice, stepped out of the car, put on some music, sat in the garden, and did a short meditation. I felt amazing.

I then decided to really plan my day. I sent energy to everything I had to do that day. One of the tasks was to go shopping for my grandson's birthday present. I visualised driving to the shopping centre, and because I also had some banking to do, I visualised myself driving around to the bank, next to the shopping centre, finding a car park there, going to the bank, and then going into the shopping centre. I visualised finding my grandson's present easily, quickly, and for under thirty dollars.

As I was driving to the shopping centre, I felt wonderful. I was really in the zone. Everything looked beautiful, and as I drove along the river, I was simply appreciating the beauty and thinking how blessed I was to live in such a beautiful place.

Just then, a song came on the radio that was so perfect. It was the Carpenters song "On Top of the World," and the words were:

Such a feeling's coming over me;
there is wonder in most everything I see.
Not a cloud in the sky, got the sun in
my eyes, and I won't be surprised if it's
a dream.
Everything I want the world to be is now
coming true especially for me.

I drove to the bank. The car park was full, but just as I turned in, a car right in front of me pulled out, so I had my parking spot. Now to find my grandson's present.

After finishing my banking, I went into one shop that had the game I knew he wanted, and it was 50 percent off, but it was still forty-nine dollars. *That's okay,* I thought to myself. *I know I will get the perfect present for under thirty dollars.*

In the second shop I went to, they had the same game for thirty-five dollars. There was also another game that I thought he'd like for twenty-five dollars. It was looking good.

However, I decided that the first game was what he really wanted, so I would just get that one. It was close enough to what I wanted to pay, so I took it to the counter, and the cashier rang it up. She said, "That's twenty-eight dollars today."

So in less than half an hour, I had found an ideal car park, done my banking, and bought my grandson's present for under thirty dollars.

It is so amazing how we can create what we want when we take the time to ask and to listen.

—Judi Mason

4

"Ask, and it shall be given you; seek, and ye shall find; knock, and it shall be opened unto you."
—Matthew 7:7 (KJV)

Finding the Perfect House

I had been using the principles of the law of attraction in my life for several years, since first learning about it in the movie *The Secret*. I think I have had an awareness of its principles for a long time, as my mum was a very enlightened person and provided me with quite a bit of freedom growing up to create (and stuff up) my own reality.

My husband's understanding of responsibility and the law of attraction came at a quicker pace. In 2007, James's armoured vehicle was hit by a roadside bomb in Iraq, throwing the vehicle some several hundred metres down the road, with him and his crew inside. Amazingly, they all survived with minimal physical wounds, but this was a huge turning point in his life.

Since that time, we became partners on a path of discovery and experimentation with the principles of creating our life in accordance with what we really want. In December 2009, James ended his career with the Australian army after seventeen years. One of the benefits of being a military family is that you receive good quality housing at a very affordable price. With James leaving the army, that was now about to end, so in early December, we moved out of our house.

Being in transition between a salary and building our own business, we determined what we could afford, and we couldn't find anything in the current market. So we made the conscious decision to become "homeless" over the Christmas period. Our homeless status was supported by my sister and her partner and by James's mum, who graciously shared their homes with us.

Interestingly, over this same period, James had purchased the book, *The Law of Attraction*, by Abraham-Hicks. He read this book and was revelling in taking onboard all of the principles of the law of attraction in his everyday life. In line with this, we sat down and made a firm decision on what we wanted in a home and what we were not prepared to compromise on. We decided that we wanted somewhere with some land so the kids could run around and we could have our little piece of nature. We wanted something comfortable, and we didn't want to pay more than $400 per week. Now, anyone who knows anything about the Canberra rental market would probably look at this description and tell us we were absolutely dreaming. Yes, we were, but we also knew that if that was what we decided we wanted, and our efforts were focused on finding that type of property, then our point of attraction would be magnetised in this direction.

While we were away, we continued to check out the rental market, but in early January 2010, we returned to our hometown, Canberra, to find ourselves still not having found a place to live. With our eldest daughter starting preschool in a few weeks, this was a cause for concern for me. It was really important at this time to trust each other, as well as the universe, and to stay focused.

Several times over the four-week period, I found myself wanting to settle for something that was not in line with what we wanted and was also more expensive, just because I wanted to regain a sense of control in my life. Can you relate to that?

The night after we returned to Canberra, we checked the rentals again, and just a few hours earlier, a property had been posted—ten acres fifteen minutes north of Canberra at $400 per week! We were absolutely gobsmacked. The next morning, we called the owner, and within a couple of hours, we were at the property. We drove onto the land and, without even seeing the house, looked at each other and said yep. It was exactly as we had imagined it.

Needless to say, the owner was very happy to sign a contract with us, and here we have been ever since. The support that we gave each other over that period was key to our success in attracting what we wanted into our life. Just having that one other person who is like-minded is a constant reminder that we are never alone, that we are always supported.

—Kirsty Greenshield

"Genius is the ability to receive from the universe."
—*I Ching*

Story Time

I attended a wedding recently, and as part of their service, one of the bridesmaids read aloud from a Dr Seuss book called *Oh, the Places You'll Go*. I hadn't read the book before, but it sounded fantastic, inspiring, and fun. I thought to myself while listening that I would like to get a copy of the book to read to my children. It would be a great one to own so we could read it over and over again.

It was less than a week later, one night while putting the children to bed, that we were deciding what to read for our bedtime story. Searching through the bookshelf, my youngest son pulled out a book and said, "How about this one?"

I could not believe my eyes, and it is giving me shivers to write this: It was a copy of *Oh, the Places You'll Go*.

I had never seen the book before, and neither had my husband. The children hadn't hired it out at the library, and we had no idea how it got into our house, but we were so thankful.

—Rebecca Malcomson

The Book

I wanted to read the book *The Da Vinci Code*, but we lived in a small country town that had no bookstores. I kept thinking that I would love to read it that weekend.

On Saturday morning, I went to a garage sale, and there it was. I love that the law of attraction works in such amazing ways. I am so grateful for the many ways, big and small, that we can create what we want.

Cash-in-a-Flash Book

I went to a seminar that featured Mark Victor Hanson as the main speaker. I was very excited because I had followed his work for a long time and read a lot of the *Chicken Soup for the Soul* books and then *The One-Minute Millionaire*, which he co-authored with Robert Allen.

At the seminar, Hanson spoke about their new book, which continued on from *The One-Minute Millionaire*. I was very keen to get the book and would have bought it on the spot, but it was not available at the time. So I waited for the release date and tried to buy it, but again, it was not available in Australia yet.

Soon after, I received an email about the book, which offered the book and the online seminar for free. I signed up immediately and received my book.

I enjoyed the online seminar so much that I ordered copies of the book for all of my children.

It is truly amazing the way the universe works: I really wanted that book, and I received it, plus so much more. But instead of buying one book, I was more than happy to buy four books for my family. The universe is always giving and receiving.

—Judi Mason

"When you visualise, you materialise.
If you've been there in the mind,
you'll go there in the body."
—*Dr. Dennis Waitley*

At My Best

I've believed in the law of attraction since I was sixteen years old. I knew that the power of the mind could make or break you. I knew that the power of the spoken work coupled with a mental thought was even more powerful. For years, I saw the outcomes of this for the good and the bad. These days, after years of practice, I've learnt to be more consistently positive and directive, which produces healthier, happier, wealthier, and more successful results. But it took years of practice. Here is one of my most notable stories.

Years ago, my husband, Paul, was working away from home. His car was very unreliable, and because he was on the road so much, we really needed another car, but at that time, we didn't have enough to buy one. I started visualising about having another car; I was putting it out there every day. About five days into the process, I heard someone talking about a website where people post things they don't want anymore and give them away free.

I jumped on the site straight away and saw there were lots of things like videos, TVs, toys, and so on. As

I scrolled down, I saw the words "Free Magna—goes well, unregistered; email me and tell me why you want the car, and I'll decide on who gets it."

Well, I couldn't believe my eyes: a free car. I immediately emailed the lady, and the following week, I received a text from her, saying, "Congratulations, the car is yours. Please collect as soon as you can."

My husband was dubious and went to collect what he thought might be a rust bucket bomb, but he called me on the way home and said, "You're not going to believe this car; it's brilliant. It even has air conditioning and power steering."

That car was so good to us; we kept it for years, and my husband drove it from the Sunshine Coast to Mackay every ten days for over a year, and it didn't miss a beat.

—Rachael Birmingham

"Jesus said unto him, if thou canst believe, all things are possible to him that believeth."
—Mark 9:23 (KJV)

Science of Getting Rich

The Science of Getting Rich was a seminar coming up in the next month that my husband and I really wanted to attend. The fact that the seminar was in Melbourne and that the tickets were going to cost about $3,000 made this dream of ours seem quite impossible, as our bank account did not display anywhere near that amount. Using all positive powers, I told everybody that we would be attending that seminar. I held this positive attitude through all the negativity that would try to get in the way of my dream.

However, even my strong positivity was weakening when it got to the Monday five days before the seminar, and there was no sign of extra funds miraculously appearing. I remained 100 percent positive (well, maybe 90 percent), when my mother, who was already booked in and attending the seminar, called with some fantastic news. She had just received an email from the organisers of the seminar about a scholarship. They were giving away eight tickets to the seminar. All I had to do was write a letter explaining why I needed to be at the seminar.

The fact was, I didn't want just one of those tickets; I wanted two, one for my husband, so my letter had to be really good. I wrote my letter immediately and sent it off.

There was nothing left to do but wait for them to call and tell me I had two tickets. I waited. Monday, Tuesday, no call. When Wednesday arrived, I was getting quite nervous. Then my phone rang. I had just won two tickets to the seminar: one for me, and one for my husband.

I was in my car when I received the call, and when I hung up, I was so excited I just sat there and screamed. I have never screamed so hard in my life. After wanting something so much and believing I would get it despite appearances, and then have it manifest in ways I would never even have dreamed of, was one of the most amazing experiences.

—Christine McLeod

"You are given the gifts of the gods; you create your reality according to your beliefs. "Yours is the creative energy that makes your world. "There are no limitations to the self except those you believe in."
—Jane Roberts
[3] The Nature of Personal Reality

Vision Boards and Books

I have had many goals in my life, but it wasn't until I started putting my goals down in the form of a vision board or a vision book that I really started seeing results. I started my first vision book about twenty years ago after reading about them. I put in it overseas travel, fine wining and dining with friends, great relationship with my husband and children, and being able to support worthy causes. Within three weeks of creating my first vision book, my husband and I had booked to attend a seminar in Malaysia. We had never been out of Australia before that, but since then, we have been to New Zealand, America (three times), Fiji, and at the time of writing this, we are about to go on a cruise around Tahiti. We have been able to donate to worthy causes of our choice, and I think we may have overdone the wining and dining bit. We have some incredible and inspiring friends, and this was just the beginning.

On my second vision board, I put in a cruise. I had always wanted to go on a cruise but had not had the opportunity to go. Again, within weeks of putting that picture on my board, I ran into an old friend who said they were going on a New Year's Eve cruise with a group, and we should go as well. When we looked into it, because of the group booking, it was very affordable, and so we booked to go. We went to Vanuatu, Noumea, Mystery Island, Palm Island, and other small islands in the Pacific Ocean. Not only that, but we were given a credit on the ship as part of the group booking, and another credit when it was too rough to land on one of the islands, so it seemed like the more we spent on the boat, the more credit we had. It was great.

I have many, many more stories of what I attracted to me throughout this book using this method, and I know this is just one way of focusing on what you want, but it does take your mind off other things happening in your life and helps you to focus on what it is you really do want. Also, I think it gets you into the creative zone, where anything is possible, and it really is.

—Judi Mason

"It's all about where your mind's at."
—*Kelly Slater, world champion pro surfer*

Surfing

This is only a small example, but one that has brought me much joy. You see, I surf. I'm not great, but I am competent, and I love it. It has provided me with hours of blissful fun, allowed me to spend quality time with my friends and brothers, and put me in touch with nature at a very real and spiritual level. So what is my example? I thought about this one day after my niece noted how difficult she finds it to get out the back. The waves break, and it is very hard to push your board through the foam, and it can be worse if there is a sweep taking you one way, and the waves constantly pushing you back. You don't get fit from surfing; you get fit from paddling out to surf.

Anyway, why is it easier for me to paddle out than it is for my niece? It's not fitness. I am sure that she is as fit as, if not fitter than, I am. It is a bit to do with experience, which helps me identify and time my route out to the back. It is also a little bit of self-belief. I have been out there before. I *know* I can do it, and my beautiful niece is yet to gain that self-belief.

However, there is one more thing: When I have paddled through the shore break, navigated my way through the foam, and battled any sweeps, there is usually one more challenge, and this is choosing the waves that I want to ride. They have power, they have speed, and when you catch them, they have beauty. But when you are on the wrong side, and you see this great wall of water rearing up at you, they are the enemy. Those waves, if they break right in front of you, will undo all your hard work and take you back closer to shore, tossing you like driftwood. I have a technique: It is like the law of attraction, though I had never thought about it like that before.

When I look up, and I think there is no way I can get through that wave before it breaks, I fix my gaze on one part of the wave. That is the part of the face that I am going to paddle through, and it will not break until I burst through and out the back of the face of that wave. I am convinced the wave will not break. My arms, already tired from the paddle so far, find extra energy and paddle harder. Where does this energy come from? Seconds ago, they felt like jelly, but my arms have a goal: to get the board through that part of the wave. My eyes stay transfixed at the spot, and my arms dig through the water and propel the board closer and closer to that spot.

The wave starts to break, but my spot is still there, unbroken on the face of the wave; the curl of the white water moves across the wave, getting closer to my spot, but so too am I. Who wins the race? Do I get to my spot before the wave bends to the forces of the sea floor, or does the wave crash on top of me, sending me hurtling back landward? Well, sometimes nature does win, but *most* times,

I get there. I burst through the face of the wave just before it breaks, and I mean just; you couldn't measure the time in milliseconds.

At that moment, my enemy is the most beautiful thing on earth. As I burst through, I can feel its power, but I also feel that at that time, just before it could pick me up and splatter me backwards, it actually helps me. The wave lifts me so that I reach my goal. The spot, the wave, my board, my body have all combined, and all have focused on that one goal: getting me through the wave and out the back.

—Scott Buchanan

"Whatever you hold in your mind
on a consistent basis
is exactly what you will experience in your life."
—*Tony Robbins*

Sandy's Story

As I write this, I feel a sense of gratitude flood my body as I gaze upon the family of wild kangaroos and their joeys feeding on the lush green grass of my property and reflect on my journey over the past five years, from welfare to millionaire.

For many years after my husband and I separated, I lived in constant struggle. I was working seven days a week in my clothing business, which I no longer enjoyed, had over $100,000 of debt, and was surviving financially through welfare. My future looked bleak, and to say I was stressed about money was an understatement.

My entire life revolved around money or, more precisely, the lack of it. Money consumed me, frustrated me, annoyed me, and scared me, and it most definitely eluded me. When it came to creating wealth, I felt powerless, hopeless, useless, and worthless. I knew deep down inside I was a good person, so why was my life such a shambles? What had I done to deserve this? What was wrong with me?

Then I discovered there's a secret to getting everything you could ever want in life. It's really simple; in fact, it may be something you have heard about or understand already. There is a law, a universal law, which states, "We attract whatever we choose to give our attention to—whether wanted or unwanted." The result of this law is this: If you continue to focus on the lack and limitation in your life, you will continue to create and attract more lack and limitation. If you instead focus on the wealth, abundance, and prosperity that is already present in your life—no matter how small it may currently be— then you will instead begin to create and attract more wealth, abundance, and prosperity.

For some people, this comes naturally. For others (like me), this can be a slow and arduous journey. Through my many money failures, mistakes, and unwise decisions when it came to practical money-making steps, I have been fortunate enough to develop a passion for what makes people rich. It is through this passion that I have been able to create my own incredible wealth, and now, I'm sharing these secrets with people across the globe.

I had used the law of attraction consciously in my life on a daily basis, however; even before I knew and understood this powerful law, it was still working in my life.

After my marriage broke up in 1990, my financial world took a turn for the worse. I had a three-year-old daughter and a six-month-old son, and with the money I received from our divorce settlement, I took out a small loan and carefully and lovingly designed and built my dream house. My plan was to live in this house until my children left home, but the universe had other ideas.

About a month before construction was complete and I was due to move into my beautiful new home, I was informed that my ex-husband's child support payments would be dropped from the expected $1,600 a month to around $100 a month. Now that was a shock. With my own business not making a profit and a now two-year-old son and a five-year-old daughter to look after, I knew this was not a good sign. Shortly after moving into my beautiful house, I simply couldn't keep up the loan repayments (even with both my sister and parents helping out) and had to put the house on the market. What a sad day that was.

When it was finally time to move out, I remember crying and walking from empty room to empty room, saying goodbye. It wasn't just my home I was saying goodbye to; I felt like I was saying goodbye to my dreams. I had hit an all-time low. With the money I had left after selling my beautiful home, I made bad investment choice after bad investment choice and eventually ended up over $100,000 in debt. I was at a breaking point. My nerves were shot. I was an impatient, angry, very sad, and stressed "crummy mummy." I had no idea where my life was going or how I would ever get out of debt. I no longer enjoyed my surf wear business but had no clue as to what I could possibly do next. The only thing that I enjoyed was personal development. "How on earth could someone make money at that?" I wondered. Little did I know what the universe had in store for me.

Two months before moving out of my beautiful home, I remember listening to an audio program.

It talked about the power between the pen and the mind, how writing unleashes a force that is far greater than your actions could ever produce by themselves and why it is so important to write your goals down. The programme I was listening to said to write down your ideal day, so I did.

What a lot of fun that was. How would my ideal day look? How would it feel? Now that was easy. "First," I wrote, "I'd get up in the morning and meditate, do some yoga stretches, and then I'd go for a walk or a run down the beach or a swim in my pool. I'd come home, get the kids off to school, and then go to the gym for a workout. Afterwards, I would read some inspiring or motivating books to help me to grow and become a better person." I remember writing all this down and saying to a friend, "If I were living my ideal day, I'd never have time to make any money." Keep in mind, at the time I wrote this down, I was over $100,000 in debt and working seven days a week in a business I no longer enjoyed. The only reason I was surviving financially was because I was receiving the sole-parent benefit (welfare) from the government. To say I was fairly stressed about money was a mammoth understatement. One thing I did to keep me sane at the time was meditating; I imagined I had loads of money pouring into my life. It made me feel anything was possible, that I could attract good into my life, that there was still some hope for my dream.

Now fast-forward about six months. I was attending a seminar for a new business I was building. The first day was business training, held by some of the leaders in the company. We were told to plan our day if we wanted to be successful; our homework that night was to fill in the day planner sheet we were given. So because I'm good at following instructions, I went back to my hotel room that night and began filling in the sheet. Now, how exactly did I spend my time these days?

Well, firstly, I get up in the morning and meditate, and then I do some yoga and go for a run down the beach. Then after I take the kids to school, I go to the gym, then I come home and read some of the personal development products I market, and then I listen to some of the tapes. Then I phone people and tell them how great the products are. Well, as you can imagine, at this point, I got chills down my spine, and I had a total "Aha!" moment. I remembered writing an identical list down months earlier, thinking it would be an impossibility, and here I was, living it. And not only was I living it, but I was also making around $10,000 a month, almost as much as I would make for an entire year previously.

It was at that moment, sitting on my hotel bed, with tears of joy and gratitude running down my face, that I realised, not just in my head but in my heart, I actually had the power to write the script for my life, that I could actually design my future. I could create it as I wanted it to be.

Now, as an international prosperity and success mentor, I've shown tens of thousands of people from around the world how to embrace and apply the law of attraction in their own lives to create whatever it is their heart desires. I have manifested some wonderful things into my life through applying the law of attraction, so I know you will get results that way. Once you are clear on what you want, and I can't say this enough, get your logical mind out of the way. Don't try and figure out how it will happen. Don't try to step all the steps through to achieving your dream. Let all that go; let the universe figure out how it will make it happen. Let the universe devise the most exciting, fun, and eventful way to make your dreams come true.

I remember having a trip to Hawaii organised to complete the last event of a three-part course with Anthony Robbins. The day before I was due to leave, I had a phone call from someone who told me about a beautiful bay about an hour away from where I was staying on Kona. "If you are lucky," she said, "you can swim with the dolphins."

I love dolphins; they are beautiful, strong, sensitive, empowered creatures. There is something magical about them that moves me whenever I see one. She told me how I would have to organise transport as well as hire out kayaks and underwater gear to get the most out of the experience. There was no time to find out all the details, but I really wanted to swim with the dolphins.

When I arrived at Kona, I made some enquiries, but the trip to that special bay was definitely in the too-hard basket. I decided to go on a local boat trip where they said we might see dolphins. I had a great day out in the ocean, diving in the warm tropical waters amongst the lava spills and brightly coloured fish, but there were no dolphins to be seen. I didn't care (much).

As I gently swayed underwater to the ocean rhythm, I imagined I could see dolphins swimming around me, and it filled me with such powerful emotions of love; it was almost as good as actually having them there with me. I still had in the back of my mind that I would love to swim with the dolphins, but with the event starting early each morning and ending very late at night, there was no chance to organise anything. Maybe I'd be able to organise it on the last day, which was a free day.

The week passed, and on the last day of the event, I was walking up the huge stairs of the Hilton Waikoloa Village and glanced up; a man walking down the stairs caught my eye and said hello. I smiled and said hello back, and then he stopped on the stairs next to me. I didn't want to be rude, so I stopped too. We chatted a little, and I told him about my ocean swim and mentioned how no dolphins had shown up.

He then told me that he lived down by a bay (the one that had the dolphins), and if I wanted, he'd love to take me there, and maybe I could see the dolphins after all.

My logical mind went into overdrive: "No way, don't even think about it." But my creative mind said, "The universe has set this up; don't let a great opportunity go by; with more than two thousand people in this hotel, you just happened to cross paths."

But my logical mind won out, and I told him I didn't think so because I didn't want him to drive all the way back here to get me (the only excuse I could come up with).

He then said, "You should; it would be perfect. I'm a yoga teacher here at the Hilton, and I have a class tomorrow morning. I could pick you up after the class, and we could spend the day there, and I could bring you back afterwards."

By this time, my hormones were winning over my logical mind as I was thinking, *Yoga teacher, good-looking, cute smile; I'm there.* So we organised that he would meet me at the front of the hotel the next morning.

At the appointed time, he pulled up outside the hotel in a fancy little red sports car. We drove away into the warm summer day, and when we reached the next town, he took me to a supermarket and told me to buy whatever I wanted for our picnic lunch. After leaving the market, he drove to a little sports store on the side of the road. When we got out, I realised we were there to hire kayaks and snorkels, goggles, and flippers to use during our day.

Oh, my gosh, I thought, *is this real? It's all falling into place so easily.*

And that's the exact thing. When you are connected, energised, and your vibration is pure and high, you will be in the flow; things will happen with little effort. Everything just seems to fall into place. That's what flow is all about; that's what being a co-creator is all about.

The yoga teacher and I had the most wonderful day in this beautiful bay. No dolphins showed up, but it didn't matter because there was no one else but us swimming amongst the thousands of tropical fish. We sat with our feet dangling in the water, munching on yummy chocolate chip cookies, drinking orange juice, and eating fresh pineapple. We spent hours talking, laughing, and really enjoying ourselves.

Now, do you think for a moment that I could have organised all those events and circumstances to happen and put it all perfectly into place? Not in a million years. The universe has tricks up its sleeve you don't even know about. You just have to be clear on what it is you want, imagine it as already real, then let it go and let the universe do its thing. Stop trying to manage the universe, and just manage yourself and your mind. The universe knows what it's doing and really doesn't need you to map out every step of its grand plan for you. It just needs you to know what it is you want, and it will work out the best way to get it to you.

And to top it off, the hotel where I was staying had a dolphin-training programme, and they had a competition where you could win a session swimming with the dolphins in their huge free-form dolphin pool. And when I returned to the hotel, I had won just that, so I got to swim with not only grown dolphins but with two baby dolphins that were only three days old. It was a magical experience, and I thanked the universe for giving me all I desired, and more.

—Sandy Forster

When You Put It Out There, the Universe Delivers

I had spent at least two years dancing around the idea of being involved in a charity that helped assist the extremely needy; however, for one reason or another, I had never made the commitment. I travelled extensively throughout the world in my twenties and still to this day love absorbing myself in new cultures and environments. I had a romantic notion to work in remote regions of the world to help others in need. My feeling now is that I was actually hesitating because I was focusing more on scarcity and not having enough for myself; you might say I was caught up focusing on material items.

It was late 2008 when I was asked to go to a function and dress like the person I envisaged myself being in years to come. When I stopped to think about this proposition, it wasn't flashy clothes or fancy jewellery that I wanted to flaunt. I actually wanted some basic toys that are affordable with wealth, such as a nice boat, a sports car, and a waterfront home. However, what engaged me deeper than any of the toys or possessions was the thought that I could contribute to a significant level and change the lives of many people who could not access the basic necessities that we take for granted.

Additionally, at this time in our lives, my wife and I had been struggling for nearly five years to start a family of our own, to no avail.

Back to the party; I had now come up with the idea that my ideal outfit to portray my success (on my terms) was khaki cargo shorts, thongs, a cap, and a white T-shirt that my wife had printed for us stating "African Hunger Project: Local business owners contribute $100,000 to the project and say it's the least they could do."

I had the keys to my toys around my neck; my wife went along with a matching outfit; however, she wore a sling with two dolls, a white doll for our own biological baby and a dark doll, signifying that we would adopt.

We relaxed and enjoyed the great company of like-minded people who were along for the night. We were asked all night what our outfits signified, and after telling the story of our dreams to raise our family as contributors to the greater community on a global level, I now had certainty that this was me; this was what I called success.

We woke the next morning to the knowledge that we now needed to get back to work, but with the ever-increasing thought that I needed to keep the feeling alive that had fired my belly the night before, when I made my deepest desires known to others.

On my second day back at work, I received a phone call from one of my clients, a very wealthy property developer, who had ties to a charitable organisation in Kenya. The phone call went like this:

"Adam, you know how we were talking about your involvement in some charity work?"

I replied yes.

He then said, "Do you want to come to Kenya with me?"

I asked, "When?" and he replied, "In two weeks."

I instantly was blown away, thinking you cannot put out into the universe what I had just done two days previously and then decline when that exact opportunity arises.

I rang my wife just to ensure she was happy for me to consider the idea; her exact words were, "Honey, you have to go; this is what you want. We will make it work financially," and for those words, I will always love her.

I rang the client back and said, "I'm in."

Two weeks later, I was in Nyahururu, Kenya, a remote region outside of Nairobi, in an orphanage that was housing 540 remarkable but needy children, mostly orphans.

My journey was only just starting, as within two months of returning from Kenya, my wife was finally pregnant. We had so many beautiful children in our lives to honour and be role models for. We feel blessed to have so many beautiful things happening to us, and we make sure we are grateful for the small things in life. My beautiful little daughter reminds me of that every day now, and I look at her mother and know what true beauty and elegance is. I feel wealthy on a daily basis now as I have so much richness in my life.

—Adam Marini

Update from Adam: After reading the few paragraphs of my story, it reminds of how many things have changed in the time that has passed. We no longer have the African equity involvement due to its winding back in 2012 after confronting several enormous challenges with government bodies and organisations that continually increased the roadblocks put up against the charity; however, we have now built an offshore business which has a strong philanthropic thread, with a training academy which helps provide opportunities to university graduates who do not have the resources to further their career. We develop them through our Six Sigma process training regime and offer the top graduates a job working for us in businesses that consult with Australian companies. The other graduates are all job ready for the other organisations that work in the outsourcing space that does not have the right training programmes to develop their potential candidates.

House Full of Furniture

We wanted to sell one of our investment homes and listed it with an agent. I know properties look better if they are "dressed to sell," so I planned to furnish the house with some furniture we already had, but it wasn't enough, and it wasn't the best style for this property. I was going to use it anyway and knew that I would have to go and buy more furniture and homewares to make this property look great. We needed to do this right away, as the agent had already booked the home for several open house displays. However, we were spending the next two days at a seminar and could not do anything before that.

At the seminar, we were talking to a friend, an interior designer, and asked where her husband was, as he was not at the seminar. She replied that he had hired a truck and was moving all the furniture from their investment properties six hundred kilometres away into storage. They had to go right past where our house was. This lady had impeccable taste and had everything necessary to dress the house for our purpose. She very kindly called her husband and diverted the truck to our property, and we all spent the day after the seminar dressing the property. This was amazing to not only get a whole houseful of furniture exactly when we needed it but also a very talented interior designer to set it up for us at no cost. The house looked great.

—Judi Mason

"Everything you want is coming. Relax and let the universe pick the timing and the way. You just need to trust that what you want is coming and watch how fast it comes."

—Abraham[i]

The Cupboard

My family and I live in a house with very little storage space, and my boys' bedroom, in particular, was always messy. We would try in vain to keep it tidy, but without a place for everything, nothing was in its place.

I looked longingly at a friend's built-in cupboards, with large sliding doors shutting away all the things we love to have but don't always need to see. My husband and I priced cupboards that were similar but not built in. The one we decided on cost $700.

Around this time, I was also trying to get a hobby of mine, sewing, to provide me with some extra income by selling children's clothing online and at local markets. It was going well, but so far, any profits I had made were going straight back into the business to buy more materials.

"Okay," I decided, "my sewing is going to buy the boys a new big cupboard."

There was a local market coming up which I had been to before and had done well at, so I thought for sure I would earn a big chunk of my cupboard money there. However, it turned out that the market wasn't as big as it had been previously. There were not as many people through the doors, and after splitting the profits with a friend of mine with whom I shared the stall, I walked away with just $140. I was happy with that. It's much more than I earn most days, but I still had a long way to go to reach the $700 for the cupboard. I was determined that I was going to buy this for my family and feel like I was helping with the breadwinning, which was usually my husband's role. So it was back to the sewing machine to earn some more money. As my brilliant mother (and author of this book) often reminds me, it's not up to me to focus on the *how*. All I need to do is focus on the *desire*.

This became very apparent one day while shopping with a friend, when I stumbled upon another cupboard. It was exactly the right size, with shelves on one side, hanging space on the other, and two big sliding doors to close it all away. The price tag on my dream cupboard was $140. I didn't make it to my target of $700, so instead, my target came down to me.

—Rebecca Malcomson

*"Speak what you seek, until you
see what you've said."*

—Anonymous

Decorating on a Budget

We were expecting baby number three and were decorating her nursery. We were on a budget and needed to find cupboards as cheaply as possible, and we also really wanted a chest of drawers. After scouring second-hand stores, we headed to the local auction, where we picked up a fantastic cupboard for only forty dollars. It needed a cleanup and some new handles, but it was a bargain, and we were happy.

Now we just needed the drawers. We headed off to get some lunch and have a well-earned break, and along the way, we passed a house that had a big pile of things in front to give away. Among them were two bedside tables, complete with three drawers each. They were a hideous pink colour, but after a quick coat of paint and new handles to match the cupboard, they were perfect and cost next to nothing. Some family members handed down a cot and changing table, and others pitched in to help paint and finish the room off. It is now my favourite room in the house and the one that cost the least to decorate.

—Rebecca Malcomson

*"Envision the future you desire.
Create the life of your dreams.
See it, feel it, believe it."*

—Jack Canfield

Vision Boards
Part 1

In June 2006, my partner and I were expecting a baby and had very little money to our name, but we desperately needed a house and a car. We wanted to own our own home, but to anyone else looking in on our situation, it would have seemed crazy. We kept focused on it, anyway. Soon after, my mother called me about a house she and my father had found for a great price in a great location. We went and looked at it, and it was just perfect for us. We never once doubted that it would be ours, and we put in an offer. Just to make sure we would get it, we went home and watched *The Secret* one more time, and then we were positive that the universe would find a way to make it ours. After much bargaining, we settled on the great price of $250,000.

Now, how to get the loan? We knew we could make the repayments but weren't in a position to get the loan, so my parents came to us and said that they would get the loan, so long as we paid all of the outgoings and took over the loan in a year's time, when we would be more financially viable. Fantastic. There's the house taken care of; now for the car. We had a few thousand saved up for our car and after looking at many cars, we finally found the one we wanted. It was in good condition and listed for $3,000, so my partner offered the owner $2,700 for it.

The owner turned around and said, "Well, to tell you the truth, we were only expecting twenty-five hundred dollars for it, so that's what I'll give it to you for."

That was unexpected but great; now we had the car. Here's the twist in the story: A little while later, we found our old goal sheet with a timeline on it, saying that in mid-2006, we would buy a house for $250,000 and a car for $2,500. We had created the whole story right down to the last dollar.

—Denielle Mason

"Every moment of your life is infinitely creative, and the universe is endlessly bountiful. Just put forth a clear enough request, and everything your heart desires must come to you."
—Shakti Gawain, Creative Visualisation[iv]

Vision Boards
Part 2

We now knew how well vision boards and goal cards worked, so of course, we made up another one, saying that our house would be worth over $350,000 a year after we bought it. Now jump ahead a year. My partner and I were talking about how we'd like to live at the beach, and if we could sell our house, we'd be able to move there. The very next day, we received a call saying that the government would like to buy our house from us for $350,000. We told the real estate agent that we thought it was worth more, and he told us that it was unlikely he would be able to get any more out of them, but he would try. He came back with an offer of $360,000, and we happily accepted. Once again, we had created our story. This time, we received even more than we had envisioned. Oh, and by the way, we are now happily living by the beach.

—Denielle Mason

"Whatever you create in your life, you must first create in your imagination."
—Tycho Photiou

I'm a Believer

I was what you might call a half-arsed believer in the power of the mind. I understood the concept, and after reading a book or watching a DVD on what could be accomplished if I just put my mind to it, I would get all excited and strut about the house, claiming my world was about to change. "I am on the way up, baby," I would announce to my girlfriend, Alethea, who had heard it all before. This positive state of mind would last about a week or so, until the next lot of bills arrived. That's when I would slip into my old way of thinking negative thoughts, and stress would flood back in and swirl around my head until I would get into a state of mind that nothing could pull me out of. "Why can't I ever have any money or get ahead? This totally sucks," I would grumble to Alethea as I slumped onto the lounge. However, recently I achieved something that I had previously perceived to be well out of my reach, and I believe this is due to the law of attraction.

An internal position was advertised on the notice board at work. This position was very attractive and very keenly sought. I thought about how great it would be to score this position but quickly dismissed the idea, as I knew there would be many more experienced people applying.

Three weeks passed, and the closing date for applications was the following day. Something in me clicked, and I decided to submit an application and put my heart and soul into getting this position. That day, I took a piece of paper and wrote: "I, Joshua Mason, will be working at —, earning $— in November 2009," and attached it to the fridge. The odd thing is that when writing this, I had no idea when the position would start, and November was still five months away. Every morning, I would go to the fridge and read aloud my affirmation and imagine working there. I even imagined what I would buy myself with the extra money I would make. I repeated this process before bed, just to make sure. At work (when I probably should have been working), I would discuss me getting the position with anyone who would listen. I was frequently reminded about the hundreds of people who had applied for the job and how slim my chances were. Normally, this would have been enough to throw me off track, but this time, I wasn't giving in so easily.

Months passed by, and I continued doing my affirmations. Something told me that this job was meant to be mine. It was just too perfect not to be. I even had other attractive job offers during that period but told them, "Sorry, I just got my dream job." Nothing wrong with a little overconfidence, right?

It was in the final days of October that I received the phone call. They wanted me to come in for an interview. It was strange because before all of my previous interviews, I would get extremely nervous, and my heart would nearly thump out of my chest, but for what seemed like the most important appointment of my life, I was cool, calm, and collected. It really surprised me. It was like everything clicked into place. I couldn't put a step wrong because my destiny had already been predetermined.

I started work in my dream job on November 7, five months after I first applied, and it is even better than I had imagined. This has been a life-changing experience, and I will never just be a half-arsed believer in the law of attraction ever again.

—Joshua Mason

"If you can dream it, you can do it."
—*Walt Disney*

Disneyland

My husband Greg and I went to America for a conference in 2002. We had our youngest daughter, Denielle, with us, and after the conference, we went to Disneyland. We all enjoyed it, but the whole time, I was thinking how much my other children and grandchildren would enjoy this, so I set a goal to one day bring the whole family over from Australia to Disneyland. When I got home, I added this to my newest vision board. I had pictures of my family surrounded by pictures of Disneyland. In 2007, fifteen of us flew from Australia to Los Angeles: our four children, their partners, and five grandchildren. When we touched down, my eldest grandson, Kobi, aged ten at the time, said, "Somebody pinch me; I can't believe this is real." Of course, one of his cousins obliged.

As well as visiting Universal Studios and touring Hollywood, we went to Disneyland for five days, and it was magical.

We would never have thought this would be possible, but having the focus and the dream really created the circumstances for us all to have this amazing and memorable trip.

—Judi Mason

> *"Nothing is impossible,*
> *the word itself says 'I'm possible'!"*
> —Audrey Hepburn

Richard Branson

This was my very first trip to Sydney. In fact, it was my first trip anywhere, by myself. I was all fired up. Sydney was where all the rich and famous people lived; I might even see one. Woo hoo. I had my hair done, bought some new clothes, and even painted my fingernails; now, that was a first. Sitting at the airport, I was thinking, *Wouldn't it be great if I got to sit on the plane next to someone who was going to the same course as me.* Well, lo and behold, I did. Amazing.

I got a window seat (my favourite) and watched the sun come up through the clouds—just awesome. It was like being in heaven, all white and silver.

Next, I was checking out the in-flight magazine, as you do, and there, right in front of my eyes, was a photo of my beautiful children. So there I was in the aisles, waving the magazine around and showing everyone who would look. A proud mother; this was just too excellent.

We changed planes at the Brisbane airport, and my feet were absolutely killing me because I had chosen shoes that looked really good but hurt really bad. Right then, I thought, *I wonder what it would be like to be paged?"* Well, no joke: It happened. They called my name over the loudspeakers and asked me to go to the luggage area. Oh, my gosh, what had I done? By now, I was convinced I was a witch. The airport staff explained I had nail polish remover in my bag, which was not allowed and could have, in fact, blown the whole plane up. Oops. Not one to waste an opportunity, I stashed the magazines into my bag and changed my shoes. Ah, that felt better. Someone was looking after me. Then, back on the plane, I was sitting next to my new friend again; excellent.

I had the very best weekend in Sydney. It was a ripper, but that is a whole other story.

However, it doesn't end there. The flight home was even more amazing. I was sitting at the airport, downing a Big Mac, when I heard someone say, "Look, there's Richard Branson, walking around just like the humans."

Hmmm, I thought, *wouldn't it be cool if he was on my flight?* Well, not only was he on my flight, but he sat next to me *and* shook my hand and signed every bit of paper I could get my hands on, as well as all the in-flight magazines with "that photo" in them and a copy of his book. He was very gracious and nice, but the poor bloke could have had RSI by the time I finished with him.

This whole incredible experience taught me that it really is true that "what you focus on is what you create. What you feel is what you attract." This is my proof.

Crikey, I reckon I could have manifested almost anything that weekend. Now to do it again.

—Lisa Dunn

"You already have within you everything you need to turn your dreams into reality."
—Wallace D. Wattles

Wishes and Dreams

Blessed with a happy and healthy life now, I was in a good place after being through some challenges, so I decided to do my *Wishes and Dreams* journal. This was the start of an amazing journey into a life of complete happiness. In this journal, I put pictures of things I'd like in my life, including a partner, travel, and a brand-new red car.

Not long after I sat down to do this, I met the most caring guy in the world, who joined me on this fascinating journey. Together, we have everything our hearts wished for, including holidays, spas, and new appliances, and I am now driving my brand-new red car. Our life is so much more rewarding because of our families and friends, and we spend long days in our beautiful garden. The grapes and mangoes are sweeter because we grew them.

We have been together now for eight years, and it was just the other day that I pulled out my *Wishes and Dreams* book and was surprised to see that all of the things I put in there are now a reality.

Life isn't always how you'd like it to be, but when you appreciate all the little things, the big things take care of themselves.

—Gladys Richards

"Man, alone, has the power to transform his thoughts into physical reality; man, alone, can dream and make his dreams come true."

—Napoleon Hill[4]

The Art of Deliberate Creation

While going through a very challenging period, I decided to write down all the problems and difficulties I was facing. As I started listing my woes and complaints, I became more and more miserable. Calling on my knowledge of visualisation, I started to write out the opposite story. For each perceived problem, I wrote down my ideal outcome. I made up a little prayer of gratitude for this ideal story and read it daily for some time.

Fast-forward to a few months later, and I read through my story again. None of it was real when I wrote it, but I am now happily (and gratefully) living in this positive reality.

—Patti Henderson

"Ask for what you want and be prepared to get it."
                                                    —Maya Angelou

Friends

My husband and I married quite young and were the first of our friends to do so. We love our single friends, and they are great to hang out with by ourselves, but we really wanted some couple friends who we would both get along with, preferably a like-minded couple with kids. This was what we put out to the universe, and the results were astonishing. A new person started at my husband's work; he was almost the same age, and they got along well. We discovered that he and his wife were expecting a child, and they had two more children at home. We were also expecting and ended up having our babies just a month apart. Their other two children were the same age as our two boys, and they get along fantastically. Now we get together for BBQs and games nights, each time discovering more and more similarities between us. We share the same birthday month. We met and married in the same year as each other. We were even at the same concert as each other when we teenagers in another city. We couldn't have imagined better people to be our friends, and all we had to do was ask.

                                                    —Rebecca Malcomson

"Believe you can and you're halfway there."
—*Theodore Roosevelt*

Swimming with the Dolphins

I have always wanted to swim with dolphins, but I didn't know where or when I would get the opportunity to do that.

One day, the company I was working with offered a prize to the top ten salespeople in Australia, for that month, and the prize was to go swimming with the dolphins at Sea World. I was so excited and determined to be in that group, although I had not achieved anything like top ten sales in the past. I worked really hard, but more than that, I could see myself swimming with the dolphins.

At the end of the month, I knew I had done all I could do, and I released the outcome. About a week later, I received the call to tell me I was in the top ten. I was so excited; I couldn't get the smile off my face for a week.

On the day of the swim, we were taken to Sea World early in the morning, before general opening hours, and led to the dolphin area. As we approached the dolphin pool, we saw that there were tables laid out around the edge of the pool, set up for breakfast. We were served a delicious breakfast while we watched our own personal show, with the dolphins swimming right alongside us. It was magical. After breakfast, we were taken to change into wetsuits, and we got into the pool with the dolphins and played with them. It was an incredible, magical experience and one I will never forget.

—Judi Mason

"Whatever you put your attention on in this life, will increase in your life. As you put your attention on Angels, they will begin increasingly to make their presence known to you."

—Denise Linn

White Light

I'd been troubled for a while, by wanting to connect with my parents, who had passed away a few years ago. I sometimes felt that they were with me. Songs on the radio and things in my life that would just happen reminded me of them, but some days I just wanted to talk to them. One day, I was browsing in a shop and found myself drawn to some affirmation cards. Whenever I see these, I always ask the question, "What do I need to focus on today?" I selected a card from the deck. The card I picked said "White Light: You have started healing." That afternoon, I was reading a great book, *We Are Their Heaven: Why the Dead Never Leave Us* by Alison DuBois, and I read about an exercise to do to "remove your pain and your worries." I was blown away by what it said.

The book explained that you lay on the bed and visualise the person you feel connected to who has passed away. Visualise them at the foot of the bed, holding a basket. Look at the basket and follow upwards to see their face. They are smiling at you, backed with a white light. The person is capable of removing your pain and worries, as they want to help you. Place your problems in their basket. The deceased have the power to take all the problems you have and will gladly do so.

So the white light message for me had double the emphasis, and I have used it over many nights, and felt at peace, connected, and dropped straight off to sleep.

—Sue Moore

The Feather

I would often find feathers, and I believed they were messages from the angels. One day, I was walking down the street and had a thought: *There's a feather,* but when I looked more closely, I thought, *No, it's only a leaf.* A more insistent thought came: *There is a feather,* but I looked again, and all I could see was a leaf. I was having this argument in my head: There's a feather; no, it's not; yes, it is; no, it's not; and so on. A little bit farther from where I was looking, there was indeed a beautiful feather. I felt that it was confirmation to trust my hunches, because obviously my conscious mind did not see a feather, yet there it was, not exactly where I'd been looking but, nevertheless, there all along.

Guardian Angel

When I drive on long trips, I always ask that the traffic will flow smoothly and that there be no semi-trailers on the road at that time, unless it's for the highest good of all. It always works and sometimes I will come up behind a semi and all of a sudden, the truck is pulling over to the side or turning the next corner. I just laugh and thank the universe.

One night, my sister and I had about a two-hour drive ahead of us on a long, dark highway. When we were about halfway there, a severe storm hit, and we could not see the road in front of us or even a safe spot to stop. Suddenly, out of nowhere, a semi-trailer was in front of us. It was a godsend, as we were able to follow his taillights all the way to the next roadhouse. When we pulled in, we looked around, but there was no sign of the truck anywhere. We were very grateful for our guardian angel that night.

—Judi Mason

Sedona Calls

When we choose to engage in the law of attraction, we really have to have enormous humility for the magical ways that the universe delivers what we ask for. The ease and grace of the flow as it unfolds is like being a participant in a dance, where the law of attraction is the leader and you, the partner who follows where the leader is taking you. The trust we give to a dance partner is the trust we hand to the universe as the very thing that we have asked for begins to manifest in our life. Where I am now can only be attributed to this trust. The belief that I have lived most of my adult life with, "If you don't ask, you don't get," was answered, as it always is, in the most magical way. In that space of total surrender to what you have asked for, all you can do is be grateful for the wonderful ways things get delivered to you.

When I became interested in creating ceremonies and rituals and facilitating meditation groups, little did I realise that this passion would take me to a place from my past that needed healing.

I lived in the United States when I was young and had no desire to return there. So I found it surprising that over a few days, I kept hearing the whispering of "Sedona. Sedona. You have to go to Sedona." I had enormous resistance, as I had never wanted to return to that country. However, the whisperings of Sedona kept coming to me.

I had connected with a person, and we were planning to create some ceremonies in Australia as a way to bring our passions and teachings to others. About a week after the Sedona calling was in my head, I happened to ask, "If there was one place in the world you would like to do ceremony with a group, where would it be?" and my friend answered, in a heartbeat, "Sedona." I was so surprised and mentioned that I had kept hearing the calling of Sedona over the last few days before our meeting.

The following day, I left home for a three-day retreat, and when I returned, my phone rang. It was my friend, saying that he had been contacted by a mutual friend, a well-known person in the States, who asked if he would be interested in doing a ceremony in America. When my friend answered yes, he was told it would be in Sedona. I was very happy for him and said I was glad he had been recognised for his worth outside of our own shores, and then he said to me, "If I go, you come with me, as you and I had just talked about this." I was very humbled. There was integrity with his reply, as well as the definite call from the universe to say, "You are going, and you are supported."

A couple of days later, with this still sitting in my heart, I was sent an email about an event: The Return of the Ancestors Gathering. It was being held in Sedona in April 2009. It was a seemingly random email.

My heart connected with what I saw, and I knew without a moment's hesitation I had to be there for that event. Sedona was definitely calling to me. This event was bringing together the leaders of many indigenous cultures to share their wisdom with the world about the changes on the earth and where the prophecies were saying the world was heading. It was a ten-day event filled with information, celebration, teachings, and sharing.

The very next day, while I was facilitating a meditation group, a new woman approached me and introduced herself. She looked me up and down and said, "Do you know that you are going to Sedona in April, and you are taking a group of people with you?"

Firstly, I was amazed and stunned, and then I went straight into, "Yeah, right; how on earth will that happen?"

She then asked, "What is the problem?"

I replied with the usual list of blockages: accommodation, transport, flights, people, and so on. This very wise woman smiled and said, "Let me make it easy for you. I own a house in Sedona that runs as a retreat centre; I will make it available for you. As for people to go with you, that's easy. Send an invitation, and they will come."

I realised that the universe was wanting me there and was creating the path with such ease and grace; who was I not to jump on this gift? I remembered the conversation of just ten days earlier where my friend and I had both said how much we would *love* to do a ceremony in Sedona, and here was the bridge already being built for us; all we had to do was take that first step. We said this out loud, and we didn't negate it; we just said that is what we wanted.

So coming home from that morning meditation, my head totally buzzing with possibilities, I sent the email about the ancestors gathering to my friend, and he immediately replied, saying, "We have to go there." I told him about all the other things that had been gifted.

We contacted our mutual friend in the States and organised for him to join us for two days in Sedona, so we could do a ceremony together with our group of people.

From the beginning of that commitment, I set the intention of having ten people with us and a waiting list by the time we left Australia.

My partner in life was so concerned about how we would get ten people to join us. Every time he mentioned his concerns, his limitations, I would stop his projections. I steadfastly held the intention: There will be ten people and a waiting list.

On the day we flew to the States, we had a group of ten and seven people on the waiting list.

My intention held strong, and I would not let fear, limitations, or scarcity affect the energy I held for this trip.

That journey was also a healing for me. A very uncomfortable memory of an event when I was young and living in America had always been in the back of my mind, so to go back there was a way for me to make peace with that part of my history.

Sedona is a place of deep healing, mystery, magic, and transformation. It called to me; I answered and held the belief that I had to be there. Now, that has become a business venture that is evolving, growing, and expanding. Sedona called to me, and it allowed me to step into a place of being all that I can be.

On the last day, after we had seen our guests off, we took a drive to Boynton Canyon, as it was a place that we felt very connected to. I noticed many PT Cruiser cars passing us, and I happened to comment to the two men with me how much I loved PT Cruisers. They were my dream cars.

One of them asked, "If you had one, what colour would you choose?"

"Definitely a black one," was my reply.

The next day, we flew into LA, and the hire car we had booked was not there. There was only one left for us to hire: a black PT Cruiser. So I finished this trip convinced that the law of attraction is a force that we can engage in. The belief, without the mental conditions and workings, will deliver what you ask for. Ask, believe, receive, and be grateful.

—Raylene Byrne

Mrs. Andersen

When I was young, like most little girls, I dreamt of growing up, getting married, and living happily ever after. Maybe unlike most other little girls, I was a bit of a tomboy, and my favourite role model was Jane from Tarzan and Jane. Consequently, I was always climbing trees and playing make-believe in my imaginary tree house.

We lived on a cattle property, and being the youngest of seven children, and with most of my siblings away at boarding school or work, and parents who were more the age of grandparents, I spent a lot of time alone. I created an imaginary world, just as I wanted it to be. I remember carving my name in the big old poinciana tree in the paddock that backed onto the house. I carved my name: "Mrs. Dymphna Andersen." I didn't know anyone by the name of Andersen, and to this day, I still don't know why I picked the name, but at that time, I decided I was going to grow up and be Mrs. Dymphna Andersen.

Well, of course, years went by, and I lost most of the adventure of my childhood; coping with reality was my primary focus. I could no longer afford myself the luxury and dalliance of daydreaming.

I went on to study economics and accounting at university, where I met the man I would marry at the age of twenty-one. I remember having a fleeting thought and recalling my childhood indulgences and thinking, *Oh well, there goes that idea. I guess I won't be Mrs. Andersen, after all.*

Another ten years slipped by. I had a busy and successful career, but things were not so successful in the marriage, and I found myself going through a very messy divorce. I was pregnant and had another baby in arms. Life became difficult, and I was once again alone with my thoughts, in a new town, with few friends or support around me, contemplating my future. The childhood dream of growing up and marrying Mr. Andersen and living happily ever after had all but dissipated.

When I started to consider the possibility of being with someone again, I admonished myself for being silly about a name. I mean, really, how ridiculous is that? But once again, I had that niggling thought that maybe there could be a next time around, and perhaps I could be Mrs. Dymphna Andersen. So I decided to make a list of the qualities I wanted in my Mr. Right.

I have always had a thing for travel, adventure, and accents, so I decided the man I wanted should be a cross between Arnold Schwarzenegger (I like the fit, muscular type) and Pierce Brosnan (I also liked the suave, sophisticated type). He had to have a regular job and be home every night, not like my previous husband, who was a pilot and away all the time. So that was my list.

Time went by. I had my second child, and the reality of bringing up two kids on my own and starting a new business (an accountancy practice) really took over my life and all of my thoughts, leaving little time for anything else.

Quite by accident, I did meet a wonderful guy, who I resisted at first. But guess what: Brian was very fit and muscular and intelligent and a little bit sophisticated. So I guess he met the Schwarzenegger/Brosnan criteria. He even had an accent; he was Danish. But he wasn't Mr. Andersen. Well, I suppose you can't have everything. We married some years later, and I become Mrs. Dymphna Boholt.

Then one day, we needed our birth certificates for something. Naturally, Brian's was in Danish, but it was pretty clear he wasn't born Brian *Boholt*. When I quizzed him as to why this was the case, he explained that he was born Brian Boholt-Andersen, and Andersen in Denmark is a very common name, like Smith or Jones, so when he was a child, his father changed their name to just Boholt, dropping the Andersen.

He was totally flabbergasted when I told him about my childhood dream and how I had carved my name in the poinciana tree as *Mrs. Dymphna Andersen*, because he had been on the other side of the world, also up a tree somewhere, playing his favourite make-believe game: You guessed it, Tarzan and Jane.

Brian has now legally changed his name back to his birth name, and I am now legally Mrs. Dymphna Andersen.

—Dymphna Boholt

*"Let us always meet each other with a smile,
for the smile is the beginning of love."*
—Mother Teresa

Mel and Steve's Story

Several years ago, I joined a women's property investing group, which brought about some wonderful changes in my life, but not quite the ones I expected. A couple of years previously, I had purchased my first home, something I was very excited about and proud of. I had never expected to be able to achieve this, as I had been a single mum since my children were five and three, having walked away from my marriage with nothing but some furniture and my beautiful daughters. I was in my mid-forties by the time I purchased the house, and as I was struggling to pay my mortgage and car on my single wage, I decided that I needed to educate myself to be smarter with my money.

The investing group was fabulous and provided lots of invaluable information and contact with like-minded women. Not only was practical investing and accounting information provided, but also processes to help with the correct mindset to achieve these goals. We were encouraged to create vision boards with photos, sayings, anything that helped us focus on our goals. The vision board was for all areas of our life we wished to change and improve, not just financial.

My main focus was both financial freedom through investing and finding a man to be my life partner. I was extremely happy with my life, but a partner to share things with would have made it perfect. You know the saying: "Things shared are double the fun."

Women from all over Australia were part of the group, and four times a year, we all congregated for a weekend seminar. By the third seminar, which was to be held at wonderful Hamilton Island, I was concerned that I was spending too much money when I should have been making money to invest. I reluctantly decided that I couldn't afford the seminar, but in my heart, I still wanted to go. In line with what I had been learning, I believed that if I were meant to go, then the universe would provide the means, so I asked the universe to help.

That afternoon, I got a $5,000 cheque in the mail from Uncle Lee. I couldn't believe it. I had the means of going to Hamilton Island. It crossed my mind that I could put this money to better use, like paying off my credit card, but I had made a deal with the universe, and I couldn't go back on my word, so happily, I went to Hamilton Island.

During a picnic lunch at the seminar, another woman, Judi, was looking for somewhere to sit to eat her lunch, so I asked her to come and join some of us on our rug. While eating our lunch, we discussed the previous session, which was about relationships. During our discussion, Judi learnt that I was single and suggested that I meet with her brother, Steve, who also lived in Brisbane. Steve phoned me, and we arranged to meet for coffee that weekend. I remember Judi telling me that Steve was quiet, and I knew that I tended to talk a lot, so I made sure I didn't dominate the conversation too much. We were instantly comfortable with each other, and the coffee became wine and dinner.

In March 2010, I married my life partner, the man from my vision board and my dreams. We have had a lot of adventures and laughs. Steve had no children of his own but became an instant Poppy when my grandchildren were born. He is a big part of the lives of my children and grandchildren, and they love their Poppy Steve.

Part of my vows was this poem by Nanushka, which is so true of our relationship:

> No shooting stars
> No softly playing violins
> Just an ordinary meeting
> On an ordinary afternoon
> But I think even then we knew
> That I would be your home
> And that you would be mine.

—Mel Buchanan

"All abundance starts first in the mind."
—Anonymous

Money Flows

After I received the idea for this book, my focus changed instantly, but I was still going through the same challenges. Several investments we had put our faith in went into liquidation and left us with just the debt, so I had been borrowing money from our other investments to prop up these and putting a lot more debt on our credit cards, just trying to get through this time. It was a strain at the end of every month to find the funds to pay for everything.

After my focus changed, I just started saying, "The money is always there when I need it," over and over again, not knowing how or where this was coming from. Almost immediately, a friend gave me a cheque for $5,000. She said she just wanted to give it to me, and I could give it back whenever I could. That immediately took the pressure off, and once that block was gone, money started flowing again. Two days after I received the cheque, I received a phone call from my accountant about an adjustment from the tax department, something I knew nothing about, and the good news was that we would be getting a refund for $5,000. That same week, I received a notice in the mail saying I could buy some options for some shares I owned. The thing is, I didn't even remember that I had these shares; I must have bought them fifteen years ago, so I was able to sell my shares, and received—you guessed it—$5,000.

Once the blocks are removed, everything can start flowing again.

—Judi Mason

"Acknowledging the good that you already have in your life is the foundation of all abundance."
—*Eckhart Tolle*

The Abundance Diary

Writing down what we want to achieve is a powerful thing. I am a financial coach, and one of the things I do is advise my clients to maintain a diary. One of my clients used the "Saved today" section in *The Abundance Diary* (a section found on each page) to manifest his income and savings.

He committed to saving one rand per day (it could be converted to one dollar a day) from the first day, adding another rand each day.

So on day twenty, he was saving twenty rands, and on day 120, he was saving R120, and day 121, R121, and so on.

He said that when he started, he had no idea where the money would come from; in fact, he entered it as a paper entry in the diary, and then when the money showed up, he saved the amount that was due, based on what he had committed on paper. Pretty amazing.

He started in April, and by November, he had saved around R25,000. He explained that he did skip a few days, here and there, but always got back on track and didn't beat himself up about it.

This is such an inspiring story.

—Linda Smith

"What you radiate outward in your thoughts, feelings, mental pictures and words, you attract into your life."
—Catherine Ponder

Fiji

My husband and I were holidaying on a beautiful island in Fiji. We were staying for a week and already had had a great turn of events when we arrived on the island. The resort had overbooked, and so we were upgraded to a deluxe beachfront apartment for the first night. Thank you, universe. Everything on the island was charged to the room, so after four or five days, I wanted to see how much we had spent so far. The receptionist asked if I just wanted the figure or a printout. I requested the figure. I was shocked when she replied that the total was just over $900, as I was hoping that the entire week would come in under $1,000 (excluding accommodation, as that was already paid for).

I am not going to pretend that I wasn't worried for a little bit and started thinking about how we would have to spend the rest of our holiday eating crackers and water in our room. But after talking to my husband, we decided that it couldn't possibly be our bill, despite appearances, and that we would have more than enough money to enjoy our holiday. So again, we went up to the reception and this time asked for a printout. The bill was only $470, almost half of the first figure we were given.

The total week ended up coming in under $1,000. This was despite the fact that my husband had taken a liking to the Fijian beer and was rarely seen without one in his hand, and I, being seven months pregnant, felt like I ate more than anyone else.

The story doesn't end there, though. When we returned to the mainland, I checked our accounts. I was amazed to find that there had been a deposit of almost $3,000 unexpectedly put into our account.

It was a truly magical holiday, and the Fijians were an inspiration on living life without worry or stress, just living in the moment. They do things in Fijian time, which means no rushing around. They are such beautiful, happy people, always smiling, and they made us feel like family.

—Rebecca Malcomson

*"It is good to have an end to journey towards,
but it is the journey that matters, in the end."*
—Ursula Le Guin

Business Class Travel

The first three times Greg and I flew to the United States, we were very uncomfortable, so we decided we wanted to be in the front of the plane. On my next vision board, I put a picture of business class travel and wrote, "Business or First Class travel."

When I was booking our flights to Tahiti, we were going through a bit of a strain financially, but I knew I had asked for business class travel, so I looked up the airfares for business class. The airline I looked up charged over $14,000 per person; I gulped and said, "I can't justify that at this moment." Note I didn't say, "I can't afford that," and I didn't give up; I had an urge to keep looking. I looked at another site that offers multiple choices of flights from different airlines, and I found business class seats for less than the cost of economy seats on the previous airline. I was so excited. I booked the flights on our credit card. However, I was a little shaky and made a mistake and had to start all over again. I was still hesitant to press the Pay button, and I had to do some self-talk to say, "This is what you asked for; now just accept it," so I pressed Pay and then realised I had forgotten to state that I wanted business class and had actually booked economy. I was being tested, so I had to contact the company and explain what had happened. They cancelled the booking for me, and I had to go through it all again.

When I looked at what we would be enjoying with business class, such as a chauffeur-driven car to the airport and back, access to the lounge between flights, comfortable layback seats on board the plane, and gourmet dining, I started to get very excited, even though I wasn't sure where the money was coming from. The very next day, I received a notice from my bookkeeper about a fairly large GST refund from the tax department. I knew we were due to receive one, but I had no idea it was so much. It was more than enough to pay for our flights. I thought this was confirmation of simply trusting. I have researched the flights since then, and nothing came up; there were no business class flights available at that price. It seems it was just there when I needed it.

Thank you again, universe.

—Judi Mason

New Car

We had two children and were trying for our third; it was really time to upgrade our car. We had a two-door sports car; it was old, rust was taking over, and we were driving on mismatched wheels because the originals had been discontinued. In fact, it was well past the time to upgrade our car.

Even with no savings to speak of, we still kept our eyes out for the type of car we would like. On my way to work, I spotted a car that seemed just right. It was a cross between a station wagon and a four-wheel drive. Not too big and not too small; it was perfect. Now we knew the type of car we wanted; we just needed the money. But meanwhile, we were booked in to go on holidays in the Whitsundays. We couldn't drive our car because we didn't think it would make it, so we hired a car for the week and left our car at home. Off we went for some sun, sand, and relaxation.

On the last day of our holiday, we received a phone call from a friend back home. There had been a flash flood, and our area was one of the worst hit. We arrived home to find that everything under our house was destroyed. The water had come up so high, the car was almost totally submerged. It had even been picked up and moved by the floodwaters. It could have been a terrible situation, but we remained positive. We knew we were insured, but we weren't insured against flooding. But still, we were sure it would all work out.

Although other people had advised us to only get the basic insurance coverage on our car, as it wasn't worth very much, we had gone for the works. Our insurance company was great; they immediately provided us with a free rental and came to collect our car to inspect it. Although we weren't insured against flooding, we *were* insured for storm damage, and that was what they deemed the flash flooding came under.

If we had tried to sell the car or even just dropped it off at the wreckers, we would have received almost nothing for it because of the state it was in. But we were covered for the market value of the car, regardless of any faults. We were amazed to receive a check for $7,000 later that week, more than we ever could have imagined. We used it to put a deposit down on our brand-new car, our perfect car.

—Rebecca Malcomson

"I don't believe in Angels, no. But I do have a wee parking angel. It sits on my dashboard and you wind it up. The wings flap and it's supposed to give you a parking space. It's worked so far."

—Billy Connolly

Car Parks

I know car parks are talked about in the movie *The Secret*, but I wanted to include my story here, as well. I have been able to manifest car parks and green lights for a long time, and I expect to get a car park just where I want it, and I do. My children also expect it because they have grown up with the law of attraction.

However, one day I was going out with my eldest daughter, Christine, to meet a friend of hers in the city for afternoon tea. We drove in, and as we arrived, another car pulled out, and we parked right outside the venue and went inside. Christine's friend could not believe we got a park outside and proceeded to mention it throughout the entire afternoon, also stating we should buy a lottery ticket because *no one* gets a park that close. We found it strange because it's become second nature to us, but then we realised that this was a reminder for us to be grateful for all of these things happening, whether big or small. So again, thank you, universe, for our car parks, green lights, and special friends to remind us of our blessings.

Another amazing car park story: One day, Greg and I were driving along a busy road, trying to find a particular building. Even though we didn't know exactly where the building was on that road, we were certain we would find a car park right outside the building. We couldn't at first see the building, but we spotted a car park and pulled in. When we stepped out of the car and turned around, we saw that directly across the road was the building we were looking for. So even though we didn't know where the building was, the universe knew exactly and provided the car park in front of it.

—Judi Mason

*"To bring anything into your life,
imagine it's already there."*

—*Richard Bach*

A Job in a Mine

My husband, Greg, has operated earthmoving machinery since he was young, and he loves it.

He always had a dream of working in the mines and operating the really big machines; he talked about it and visualised it. He could see himself operating those machines.

At that time, it was an almost impossible dream because very few people outside of the mining industry got into the mines. However, he had a dream, and he wouldn't let that minor fact deter him, so when a position became available, Greg applied. He was feeling a bit nervous about it, and I said to him that he had done all he could; now he should just throw it up to the universe, meaning, just let it go.

A little while later, I walked into our bedroom, and he jokingly said to me, "You almost caught me throwing up."

There were over 850 applications and only five positions available. Greg was one of the successful applicants, with the other four all coming from within the mining industry. He beat the odds because he believed he would. The law of attraction at work again.

—Judi Mason

Career: Working at a Winery

While I was in my twenties, dreaming of things I'd like to do when I was older, I thought it would be pretty cool to own a winery and make organic wine. That just seemed like a daydream at the time, growing up in England.

A decade later, I moved to Australia, and I was looking for a part-time job in marketing. I looked on the internet and found the perfect job: a twelve-month maternity leave contract working part-time as a marketing manager for three days a week at a winery.

Although the closing date had already passed, the job was still advertised, so I applied. I followed up with a phone call two days later and was told I had an interview. I was offered the job the next day. Excellent. It just goes to prove that when you have those inspired thoughts, you should follow them through.

—Sue Moore

"Anyone who lives within his means suffers from a lack of imagination."
—Lionel Stander

Dinner for Two

Several years ago, Greg and I were living on the Gold Coast in Australia. We had a toddler and a baby, and we were struggling financially, just living from week to week. It was Greg's birthday, and we had no money to spare, but I wanted to do something special for him. Without even knowing about the law of attraction back then, I imagined going out somewhere nice for dinner, even though I didn't know how.

A little while later, I was listening to the radio, and they were doing a promotion for Pisces Seafood Restaurant and were giving away a dinner for two to the first caller. I called, and I won the prize. I then organised my sister-in-law to babysit.

When I rang Greg to tell him we were going out for dinner, he immediately panicked, saying, "We can't afford that!" (a phrase now banned from our household).

So I told him how I'd won it; he was very excited and couldn't believe how lucky we were.

I had a strong desire to do something special; I had no idea how that was going to happen, but I put it out there and let it go. The universe did the rest.

We had a beautiful meal, and it was an exceptional night to remember.

—Judi Mason

*"There are always flowers for those
who want to see them."*

—*Henri Matisse*

Bouquet of Flowers

I was busy with housework and thought how nice the house would look if I brought some flowers inside. A few minutes later, there was a knock on the door. My lovely neighbour from across the road was there with a bouquet of flowers for me.

—Patti Henderson

Flowers

Recently, I was sitting at my computer, thinking, *I would really love some flowers. I'll see if I can manifest a bunch of flowers.* Within five minutes, I received an email from a friend in the United States, with a beautiful bunch of flowers on it, saying "Just thinking of you."

The law of attraction works in amazing ways.

—Judi Mason

*"The future belongs to those who believe
in the beauty of their dreams."*
—*Eleanor Roosevelt*

Piggy Bank, Flowers, and Other Things

One day in November, I was feeling less than abundant and decided to make another vision board, as it always helps me to focus on what I do want, and it is lots of fun choosing the pictures, cutting, and pasting. I was going through magazines, including a finance magazine that I was sent earlier in the year. In it, there was a picture of a piggy bank, a gold one with Chinese writing on the side to symbolise the year of the pig in Chinese astrology.

I remembered that when I received the magazine, I really liked that pig and had looked everywhere for one like it. I looked in market stalls, Chinatown, and different states throughout Australia, but I could never find one even resembling this one. I was attracted to it not only because the pig looked rich and abundant, but also because the pig is my sign in Chinese astrology. I had forgotten about the golden pig until I came across it as I made my vision board, and I decided to put him on the board.

I included other things, including a bright orange flower in the middle of my board. My daughter asked me why I had put the flower there, and I said, "Because it just looks pretty."

The very next day, my husband, who had been away for a few days and hadn't seen my new vision board, brought home a bunch of flowers, and right in the middle of the bunch was a bright orange gerbera, exactly like the one on my board.

Later that same day, we went out to buy groceries, and I felt drawn to go into a little novelty store, and right there on the shelf was the *exact* piggy bank that I had put on my vision board the day before. It had no price on it, but I picked it up and walked to the counter, saying to myself that it didn't matter what it cost because it was a symbol of my abundance.

The girl behind the counter said, "That's three dollars, please," and I almost laughed out loud and happily paid for my pig.

—Judi Mason

"Until one is committed there is hesitancy, the chance to draw back, always ineffectiveness. Concerning all aspects of initiative (and creation), the ignorance of which kills countless ideas and splendid plans: that the moment one definitely commits oneself, then Providence moves too. "All sorts of things occur to help one that would never otherwise have occurred. A whole stream of events issue from the decision, raising in one's favour all manner of unforeseen incidents and meetings and material assistance, which no man could have dreamed would have come his way."
—W. H. Murray

This Book

To put together this book, I wrote many of my own stories and collected many stories from friends and family of all ages, from children to great-grandmothers. I was continually receiving beautiful, positive feedback about this book, and everyone who was contributing was commenting on how great it was to remember their stories, and how it reminded them to focus on what they want to create. Then the book ground to a standstill. I still needed more stories to complete it, but I had not set myself any deadlines, so it just faded into the background of what I was doing.

At the start of this year, my husband and I decided to do a vision board for the year, not our usual generic vision board, but a much more focused one. The castles and private jets were left off, and we focused specifically on what we wanted for this year. On my board, I focused on my main goals: I wanted to set up a website (which I had no knowledge about at all), and I wanted to finish my book. This meant I had to get out of my comfort zone and start asking a lot more people to contribute stories. I started going to networking lunches with postcards I had printed out; I sent emails to lots of people asking for their help, for their stories and to pass the email onto their contacts.

Once I set the deadline and started taking action to make it happen, I was inundated with opportunities, and I met people with the skills to help me to achieve my goal. It was just amazing. There is no limit to the possibilities out there. I was actually feeling overwhelmed by the abundance of opportunities pouring down over me (that's what it felt like). I was sent emails about competitions for spiritual authors; I was invited to contribute stories to other compilation books. I met people who knew about websites, marketing, and selling books; I was sent information on courses I could do to help with the direction I was taking. I talked to people who knew people who could help me with editing, book cover design, and printing. Ask, and you shall receive.

—Judi Mason

"The universe is always speaking to us ... sending us little messages, causing coincidences and serendipities, reminding us to stop, to look around, to believe in something else, something more."

—Nancy Thayer

Synchronicity

Life sometimes serves us a curveball, one that we can either run from or run with. For me, I caught my curveball, and I am still running with it. Living in the moment and guided by spirit, I find myself living frequent moments of synchronistic events. Some seem to stick in my memory more than others. In 2005, I was travelling with a friend. As we drove, I was talking about the power of music and singing about my ancestors. My friend decided he wanted to share with me a piece of music by a Hawaiian singer. He stopped the car on the highway and searched through his CD collection, but when he finally located the correct case, he opened it only to find the CD missing. Two hours later, upon arriving at our destination, the home of another friend, there sitting on the bench was the same CD, waiting to be played.

I have had many deep synchronistic moments; here is what I believe is the best: In 2004, I had my first solo art exhibition in Darling Harbour, Sydney. I sold a painting to a couple; the painting was titled *Yulpu Ceremony*. It was about the first time I ever sat in ceremony with my grandfather. The couple had been travelling in Australia for several weeks, and this was their last destination. When they purchased the painting, I asked them for their details, as I wanted to be able to visit this painting sometime.

Fast-forward twelve months, and I was without anywhere to stay upon arriving in Los Angeles, so I called the couple who bought my painting. They were surprised to hear from me but came and collected me from the airport. Upon arriving at their home, they opened their front door. Right in front of me was a didgeridoo I recognised immediately; I had made it and sent it to a shop in Darwin. They had purchased this didgeridoo from the only shop in Australia that sold my instruments, two weeks before meeting me at my art exhibition in Sydney. This instrument was plain, no artwork, but they said it called them. Further to this, on the wall of their guest room was a photograph of an old Aboriginal man. It was my grandfather's brother, my uncle. They had taken this photo at the beginning of their Australian tour, three weeks before meeting me in person.

Stories like this make you realise the divine flow that exists when you can truly surrender to spirit. This couple now own the largest collection of my artwork. They have also become like a mother and father to me.

—Jeremy "Yongurra" Donovan

Karate

It was time to take my son to his weekly karate lesson when I realised I didn't have the ten dollars needed for the fee. Almost immediately, I had a vision of opening my car door to find a ten-dollar note on the ground. With the certainty that I would have the money needed to pay for the lesson, we headed off. The whole way, I held that clear vision of the ten-dollar note lying on the ground beside the car. When we arrived, I opened the car door, expecting to find the ten dollars, only to find nothing lying on the ground. I must admit I felt crushed; I was so certain it would be there.

As I was trying to get over my bruised ego and figure out what to do, a shout came from my son: "Mum, I just found ten dollars lying next to the car." I was speechless. "I don't need it; I think you should have it" were the next words that came from my nine-year-old boy. He had no idea that I needed money for the lesson and would have normally taken that money and bought as many lollies as he could get his hands on.

—Christine McLeod

"Money is usually attracted, not pursued."

—Jim Rohn

Scratch-Its

When I went to the local newsagent to buy some milk, I saw that they had the latest issue of a magazine that I liked; however, after I paid for the milk, I only had one dollar left in my wallet. The magazine cost five dollars. I had a hunch to buy a one-dollar scratch-it ticket, and I somehow knew that I would win the money for the magazine, and that's what I did. I bought a scratch-it, won five dollars, and bought the magazine. I have done this a few times since, with the same results.

—Judi Mason

"The impossible is possible when people align with you. When you do things with people, not against them, the amazing resources of the higher self within are mobilised."

—*Gita Bellin*

What's in a Name?

One of the hardest things to decide when starting a new company is what to call it. My business partner and I spent three months doing just this, trying to decide on a name for our training company. For three months, we tossed around various names. I didn't like the names he came up with, and he didn't like the ones I thought of.

One morning at a customer site, we both walked past the tearoom, and in the middle of the table was a sign that read "Think Safety." I turned to my business partner and said, "That's it: Our company name is going to be Think Training." My business partner did a quick search but then informed me that we couldn't have that name, as it was already taken. There was something about this name that as soon as I said it out loud, I knew without a single doubt that it was to be our new company name. I also knew I would sort out this minor detail of the name being taken. The picture I had was very clear: I could see the name on the office door, I could see the letterhead, I could see the business cards, and just ten minutes later, when asked what our company name was, I said, "Think Training."

The very next day at the accountant's office, I told him our new company name. I mentioned the name was taken, but I knew he would sort this out. I had a certainty when saying this because I truly knew this would happen. The accountant looked at me and said, "Just wait a minute," and left the room. He came back moments later and proceeded to inform me that the company Think Training was one of his clients. The lady who owned the company name didn't run it as a business and was just using it as a trading name. There are hundreds and thousands of accountants throughout Australia; what are the odds that this company name was known to my accountant, and he did their books?

Two days after leaving the accountant's office, we had purchased the company name for $2,000.

—Allison Pooler

"Everything is Energy and that is all there is to it. Match the frequency of the reality you want and you cannot help but get that reality. It can be no other way. This is not philosophy. This is physics."

—Albert Einstein

Mr. Universe to Master Manifestor

My husband, Greg, used to joke that he was Mr. Universe because I would say the universe will provide, and he said he'd have to go to work to get the money for the things I wanted; therefore, he was Mr. Universe.

One weekend, we went away to an island with some friends. Greg said, "I hope it's not too hot," and in moments, the clouds came out, and it started to rain. He then said, "I hope the rain clears so we can go snorkelling," and right on cue, the rain cleared.

My girlfriend and I were lying in the shallow water, drinking champagne (as you do on tropical islands), and we kept asking our husbands to fill up our glasses. After doing this repeatedly, the guys started to get sick of it, and Greg said jokingly, "I hope a shark comes along." A few minutes later, some people at the other end of the beach started pointing and saying they thought they'd seen a shark. It was then we started calling Greg the "Master Manifestor."

Now he is always manifesting things he needs, right when he needs them. Recently, he was about to do some tiling, but he had lost his adhesive mixing bucket. He thought, *I'll have to buy another one,* then thought, *No, I'll just find one.* The next day, he was driving along, and there was a bucket sitting on the side of the road. It had obviously been used as a tiler's mixing bucket. A few steps further on was a five cent piece; he is always finding five cent pieces, and to him, that was just confirmation of the law of attraction.

Another example of the Master Manifestor at work involves gardening. We wanted some garden edging, and so Greg suggested we go to a garage sale. I thought, *What are the chances of the only garage sale in a very small town having exactly what he wants?* But when we arrived, Greg walked straight over to a pile of garden edging and bought it. He just *knew* he would get what he wanted. He does this when he needs something specific; he always expects it, and he always receives it.

—Judi Mason

Influences

This story is about how other people can influence our thoughts, sometimes negatively, but thankfully, there are a lot of positive influences, as well. I had received a notice in the mailbox saying I had to collect a registered letter from the post office. I was so excited. I would head there right after work to see what treasures were coming my way. When I arrived at work, I mentioned to my boss that I had a registered letter to collect. She replied that it was probably a speeding fine because they always come by registered mail. Well, that quickly deflated my happiness, and suddenly, I was dreading going to the post office.

My father was in town at the time, and that afternoon, he came and collected me from work. I asked if we could drop past the post office to collect my letter and mentioned that it could be bad news and I was a little worried about it. My dad is an amazing manifestor, and he quickly put me back into the right frame of mind, saying how he thought it was going to be something great because most people send valuable items by registered post. With my mind back on track, I almost skipped into the post office and reappeared with a letter in hand. Excitedly, I opened it and found a letter from a beautiful friend, saying how she had been reading up about tithing and thought that both my husband and I were inspiring; she felt compelled to send us a cheque for $300.

—Rebecca Malcomson

Rainbow Seekers

Driving through the rain and sunshine one day, around Mount Beauty, in the alpine region of Victoria, Australia, I mentioned to my husband that we might see a rainbow soon. We turned the next twisting bend, and there it was, straight across the road in our path. "Wow," we both said, in awe of its beauty.

"Darl, you're getting good at this," my husband said. We both smiled, and then, as we twisted and turned down the mountain, we saw it again another three times, from different angles.

The most spectacular sighting was when we arrived at Sullivan's Lookout; the clouds cleared, and we saw the valley down below us with a vibrant rainbow.

—Sue Moore

> *"Every single second is an opportunity to change your life, because in any moment you can change the way you feel."*
>
> *—Rhonda Byrne*

Motorbike Trip

I was working on an excavator when a ute drove past me with a couple of motocross bikes on the back and a couple of guys in the front, obviously heading off for a ride somewhere. I was feeling a bit jealous and started to curse, but then I thought, *No, good luck to them; isn't it great for them to be going off for a ride and enjoying themselves?* I started visualising myself going riding, and within five minutes of that happening, I received a phone call from a mate I hadn't seen for a while to say that he and a couple of guys were going riding that weekend and would I like to come as well? Of course, I said yes.

—Greg Mason

"As far as I can tell, it's just about letting the universe know what you want, and then working toward it while letting go of how it comes to pass."
—Jim Carrey

Our Home and Mentor
Part 1

Greg and I travelled a lot to the Sunshine Coast and decided we wanted to move there, so we sat down and wrote out what we wanted in a house:

- walking distance to the beach
- close to restaurants
- ability to renovate (we wanted to be able to increase the value of the property)
- have a pool
- open plan
- three or four bedrooms
- an office
- easy to afford
- around the Marcoola area

We started looking on the internet and found a property that was going to auction, but we usually don't like auctions, so we didn't look too closely at that property. I talked to real estate agents, and one informed me about a house that came up for sale in the area we wanted. We were told there was a high demand in this area, and the property would be sold quickly.

The house was within walking distance of the beach, it was close to restaurants, it needed renovation, and it was affordable, but it had no pool. We decided we could put a pool in and it was worth the eight-hour drive to inspect the property. The house going to auction was just four houses away from this one, so we thought we would also have a look at it while we were there. It had all of the above *and* a pool.

When we looked at the first house, we decided we could not add much value to it, as it was just a beach shack; rather than renovating, you would need to knock it down and start again. The auction house, however, had a lot of potential, but the agents told us they were expecting a high price at auction. I said I would not bid at auction. I knew if it was meant to be our house, we would get it after the auction. The agent thought there was no chance that this house would not be sold at auction, but I told him to call me if it wasn't.

I added that house to our vision board and visualised living there. On the day of the auction, we were away, so some friends went to view the auction. Apparently, only one bidder turned up, and the reserve price was not met. After negotiating with the seller, we were able to buy well below the reserve price and are now living in our home, walking to the beach every day, and we have started renovating. It is a great house in a great position, and it's going to look amazing when we finish the renovations. We got exactly what we asked for.

—Judi Mason

Our Home and Mentor
Part 2

I had read a lot of books about investing and personal growth, and in many of the books, the benefits of having a mentor, someone who has achieved what you want to achieve and can teach you and make you accountable, were mentioned. I sat down and thought about who could be my mentor. I chose someone I admire and with whom I had already done some seminars. Dymphna Boholt is a property millionaire, investor, accountant, author, teacher, and an amazing woman. I gathered up all of my courage and rang her up to ask if she would be my mentor. She was very polite and flattered but would not commit at that time, but as I had also read that you had to be persistent, I didn't give up.

A while later, I went to an advanced seminar put on by Dymphna, and when she asked how I had enjoyed the seminar, I replied that it was awesome, but I still wanted her to mentor me. She laughed but, again, did not commit. Sometime later, we were attending yet another seminar put on by Dymphna, and at the end of the seminar, she announced she would be doing a personal mentoring programme for a select few people; later, she looked at me and said, "This is your fault." I was thrilled. I applied and was accepted into her programme.

After we had been living in our new home for a few months, I started to unpack a box that had been sitting there, and in it, I found a vision book

I had written in about twelve months previously. I had written, "We are now living in our new home on the Sunshine Coast and are being mentored by Dymphna Boholt." At the time I wrote this, I had no idea that this would happen. Since then, Dymphna has not only been a wonderful mentor, she has also become a very close friend.

—Judi Mason

Upgrade and Free Wine

We went on the luxurious six-star Abraham cruise around Tahiti and had an amazing time. We had booked a room in a brand-new resort in Papeete for our last night before flying back home. At the time I booked it, I took the cheapest room option because I knew we would have already had a great week, and this was just a stopover. However, on the cruise, Abraham talked about "when you expand, you can't go back."

On the cruise, we met some fellow passengers who had stayed at the Papeete resort, and they let us know that even though the resort was beautiful, because it was so new, it did not yet have a liquor licence. It was not close to any other restaurants or shops, so if we wanted to enjoy a drink, we would have to make sure we took some with us.

On the final night of our cruise, after partying on the deck and saying goodbye to all of our new friends, we went back to our cabin to find two bottles of wine with a note, saying, "To you amazing creators, manifesting wine for your stay at your resort." That was a very nice surprise, but it was just the beginning. When we arrived at the resort, even though they were fully booked (everywhere in Tahiti was fully booked for the Quicksilver Pro Surfing Competition), the concierge said, "We have a surprise for you," and upgraded us to their best room, right on the waterfront, overlooking the pool. It was beautiful and a fitting end to an incredible week.

—Judi Mason

Less Is More

Or, attracting less into my life and enjoying it more.

From the mid-1980s until around 2000, I had constantly battled with my weight, trying diet after diet every year and becoming more and more convinced I was destined to be fat, that it was a genetic condition I could not overcome.

It is soul destroying to accept the role of victim and to feel totally out of control when it comes to your own body and health. I was successful in business; in fact, I was asked to speak on health and business issues in several countries. I had a happy marriage and four wonderful daughters. I should have felt empowered and grateful. Instead, I felt like a total failure. I felt that I was going nowhere, simply because on a very intimate and personal level, I was totally out of control. I had succumbed to being a fat victim, without hope of a solution anywhere in sight.

By around 2000, I had decided that it was just too damaging emotionally to attempt any more diets and that I would just get used to being fat as part of my makeup. Making this decision achieved two things for me:

1. I felt somewhat better as a result of not experiencing constant failure when dieting.
2. I became fatter and fatter, since my attitude simply attracted more body fat.

In 2005, I was at a trade show and was speaking with a lady who told me an amazing story of how she had lost more than thirty-five kilos quite quickly; she had kept it off and felt so much healthier. To this day, I do not remember her name, but I owe her a debt of gratitude, as in the course of a fifteen-minute conversation, she completely messed with my "victim acceptance" mentality. She was living proof that if she could change, then so could I.

Over the next ten days, I redesigned my mindset. I had long known about the law of attraction and had used it in setting business and family goals. I now focused on attracting ways that would help me to become motivated enough to lose the weight forever and also for a method to achieve this. I no longer felt like a victim. I was now more like a seeker or traveller, looking for an answer.

Within days, I was in Indonesia to speak at the launch of a new nutritional supplement. The organiser had arranged for myself and two doctors, who were also speaking at the launch, to stay together in a luxury three-bedroom hotel suite. During our free time around the launch event, we played tourist, and both the doctors watched me struggle to lug my 130-odd kilograms around in the tropical heat. They looked on as I plugged in my breathing apparatus at night to help me sleep with sleep apnoea (a common sleep disorder amongst obese and overweight people). They both took turns in gently advising me to lose weight before something serious occurred.

After I had spoken and given what I thought was a great seminar (modest as ever) to around 150 Indonesians, I stepped down from the stage, and as I began to leave the room, I was accosted by a very irate lady who literally poked me in the chest whilst loudly telling me, "You, you are a disgrace; you talk about health, but you are fat, fat, fat!"

Talk about humiliating. To have this happen as many of the audience listened was horrendous, and I remember going next door to the bar to recover with a drink. But the day was not over yet; that night, I had arranged dinner with a good friend from Perth, who was also in town on business. We settled into a fantastic Chinese dinner, but later that night, he leaned across the table to tell me that he was really concerned about my health, that I looked *terrible*.

Well, I had wanted to attract the motivation to lose the weight into my life, and here it was, hitting me like a hailstorm, fast and furious. I felt terrible, but I also knew, not thought but *knew*, that I would turn my health and my weight around forever. It was the first time in my life I was ever so totally sure of something. Now I just had to focus on attracting a method to achieve it, but strangely, I felt it would come now that I was ready. I went to sleep more peacefully than at any time in years.

Upon returning to Australia, I had a message from an old friend who wanted to catch up for a coffee. He was one of the top doctors in Australia, working with environmental medicine and gut health. Since I had not heard from him for some time, this was a great chance to speak with him about weight loss ideas. I prepared for our meeting by purchasing books about several of the more reputable diets on the market, with the idea that he might review them and let me know which one to do.

As we sat and chatted, I told him that I was going to become slim and that it was not a maybe but simply a matter of picking the most effective method. He looked quite sceptical but agreed to review the programmes I had brought along. I thought he would take them home and spend hours checking them out, but he merely flicked through them and dropped all but two onto the floor of the restaurant, declaring they were "totally useless and likely to almost guarantee I would not succeed, that they had no science at all." As for the other two, he said they were okay but that he could design something that would work at least 30 percent better. It was a revelation to me; here was a guy I had known for more than a decade, and I had never even asked him about weight loss.

Suddenly, now that I was focused on attracting a solution into my life, he showed up (in fact, *he* had contacted *me*), and at our social catch up, he offered to design a custom-made programme that would not only get the weight off but enable me to keep it off and improve my health.

To say I was amazed would be an understatement. Within a week, I had lost several kilos, and twenty-three weeks later, I was forty-three kilos lighter. Five years on, I retain my lower weight, my health is massively improved, and I am fitter now than when I was twenty-five.

Not only did I attract the people to motivate me to do it no matter what, but I also attracted someone to help me with a simple system to make it work. In addition, I attracted a team of great people around me who together have designed and built a truly revolutionary weight loss system that has helped thousands of people to successfully lose weight and improve their lives. I also attracted people who helped me to write a bestselling book on the weight loss industry that has been read by tens of thousands of people.

I cannot express the gratitude I feel and the power I now understand lies within us all to attract whatever we need into our lives. I see people every day attracting mediocrity and unhappiness, ill health, and disease. However, I see many, many others who are attracting amazing happiness, health, and success in their lives.

The truth is that we *will* attract things, people, and events into our lives. The question is, will we attract great people, great things, and great events, since that is just as easy (and much more fun) as attracting negativity and mediocrity?

I wish for you a life of attracting only the best into your life; may the force be with you.

—Graham Park

*"To enjoy good health, to bring true happiness
to one's family, to bring peace to all, one
must first discipline and control one's own
mind. If a man can control his mind he can
find the way to Enlightenment, and all wisdom
and virtue will naturally come to him."*

—*Buddha*

Health: Believe You Can

In October 2014, I was training for my first marathon. Two weeks out from the event, I suffered a bad migraine that lasted five hours. I eventually went to sleep through the pain, but I woke up with numbness down the right side of my leg. I was unable to feel my foot, and I had tingles through my back.

After a month of tests and scans, I was told I had eight lesions on the brain and received a diagnosis of multiple sclerosis (MS). My neurologist recommended that I take a course of drugs "that might prevent future attacks happening, and then, they might not." That sounded like playing Russian roulette to me, especially with the side effects of the recommended medication.

So I looked for an alternative. I had heard of other people healing themselves from incurable diseases, and I thought if they could do it, so can I. I believed that if I created MS in my body, I could also un-create it.

I researched online and completely turned my life around. I improved my diet by cutting out gluten, dairy, and sugar; started meditating daily; had regular kinesiology sessions; and reduced stress from my life.

During my daily meditations, I mentally rehearsed being in the neurologist's office during a future appointment. I imagined the conversation with him and looking at my brain scans before with eight lesions and after with none.

During this time, I coaxed my body back to start running again. Nine months later, I crossed the finishing line of the Gold Coast Marathon. A month after this, I returned to see the neurologist, and he told me, "Out of the eight lesions, most of them have completed disappeared, and the rest have significantly diminished." This was through no medical intervention at all.

This was also exactly how I imagined it. So believe you can do anything, and you will.

—Sue Moore

> *"The secret to making something work in your
> life is, first of all, the deep desire to make it
> work; then the faith and belief that it can
> work; then to hold the clear definite vision in
> your consciousness and see it working out step
> by step, without one doubt or disbelief."*
>
> —Eileen Caddy

The Song: "Everything's Alright"

I was going through some health challenges and had just been to see the doctor, and even though I like to be positive and focus on health, doctors like to tell you everything that is wrong and could go wrong, so as I drove home, niggly little doubts and fears kept popping up. I said a prayer to the universe, God, source (whatever you like to call it), and I asked for a sign to let me know I was going to be alright and also that when I got the sign, I would know it without a shadow of a doubt. Later that day, I got into the car, and the song that came on the radio as soon as I started to drive was "Everything's Alright" from the musical *Jesus Christ Superstar*. I knew in that instant that that was my answer. I knew it without a shadow of a doubt, and now whenever I start to doubt or have fears, that song pops into my head and I start singing it:

> *Try not to worry, try not to hang onto
> problems that upset you, oh,*

Don't you know everything's alright, yes everything's fine, and we want you to sleep well tonight.

   About a week after I heard the song, I went for a walk to a beautiful creek but then had to walk back up a very steep hill, and as I was still having some health challenges, I was struggling to get up the hill. I was out of breath and stopping every few minutes. I got about halfway and felt like I couldn't go any farther; there was a seat quite a bit farther up, and I told my husband to go ahead to wait for me there, as I needed time alone to refocus. I stood there and breathed deeply, and once I caught my breath, I just started singing the song. As I was singing, I started to walk, and before I knew it, I had caught up with my husband. I don't even know how I got there so fast; it was like I was carried. I felt wonderful. We still had farther to walk, and it was probably the steepest part of all, but I did it effortlessly and arrived back up at the top, feeling great and not out of breath at all.

   Isn't it an amazing universe we live in?

—Judi Mason

Doubts

I was having a bad day, a moody day. I started having doubts about this whole law of attraction thing. "It's not real," I said to my sister. "It doesn't work. When it does work, it's just because of a coincidence."

She knew I was just having a bad day and letting off steam. "You will see," she replied. "Something will happen, and you will know it's real."

Later that day, I went to the library and looked at cookbooks. I had been watching a cooking show on television and was inspired to try more things. There was nothing very interesting there, though. The next day, I went to the shops and saw a cooking magazine. But as I am a vegetarian, it didn't really have anything I could make in it. I thought that maybe I would print some recipes off the internet and put them in a binder, but I didn't get around to it.

That same week, my friend asked me to attend a movie premiere with her. When we arrived at the theatre, we were given gift bags with assorted items in them as a thank you for attending. My gift bag contained a fashion magazine, some chocolates, and a vegetarian cookbook.

I laughed out loud. Universe, how could I have ever doubted you?

—Rebecca Malcomson

Masterful Manifestations

I had a quote come through this morning. Nothing unusual in my world, even as my partner and I are enjoying the fourth day of our Abraham-Hicks South Pacific Island cruise. Today is our first day off the boat, and we are due to step off onto the island of New Caledonia. So much is happening moment by moment that the space to write it down and share my usual writing into my books or via Facebook did not eventuate. I will get around to sharing my quote shortly, but first let me fill you in on what happened as the words kept percolating through me regardless, alongside the recent days' events that culminated in a perfect, juicy rendezvous.

With so many activities, events, and fine dining experiences on board the *Celebrity Solstice* in the last few days, my photographer partner, Douglas, had attempted on several occasions to get someone to take a photo of the two of us, using his professional camera. Nevertheless, no one seemed to possess the skill to take a good photo, and in some cases, they couldn't even press the camera button after repeated attempts. It was rather amusing. But what was even more astonishing was the perfection of this rather bizarre contrast in setting us up for an exquisite manifestation.

This morning before we left the boat, I shared with Douglas how I wanted to connect with Esther Hicks, one of the world's most prolific law of attraction teachers, and the reason we came on this cruise. I wanted a connection that was physical and tangible. My desire was to connect through a hug, with our eyes, and through my feeling of appreciation (the energy more so than any words).

He piped up with a logical, "The only way will be to get into the hot seat."

Here, you put your hand up when invited, alongside, in this case, another thousand people, out of which only one gets selected to sit in the hot seat and ask a question. Then, Esther speaks from her higher self to yours in answer to your question. In fully receiving the message, it is designed to activate a shift to your highest vibrational frequency.

When Douglas expressed his view that I would have to get into the hot seat to manifest my desire, I replied emphatically, "No! It's so much more than that." I really appreciated the contrast in his words, which helped me immediately further clarify exactly how I desired the meeting to occur.

We then got off the boat, and I felt enthralled in our day's adventure and excited by what we would see and where life would take us. We proceeded to one of the last main stops along the beach road, as we followed our flow. We walked along one of the beaches for quite a way, away from it all really, until we stumbled upon a restaurant out on the ocean, with its own pier. It was totally drawing us. I grabbed Douglas's camera and took advantage of the unique scenes, the beautiful features along the pier, and the juicy environment. It was as though I was using a camera and merging with all the detail of my magical environment for the first time. Yum.

I spent a long time absorbed in taking photos. I also became aware of how I was in the same inner state of connection that my unwritten quote was describing. The words resurfaced delightfully again, at this moment:

> "When you place your full attention on your connection with your Inner Self, there's no need for any attention from the outer world. The rendezvous with your God Essence is exquisite beyond measure. And then you get to rendezvous with others who know their God Essence too."

I smiled knowingly, and soon after, we left the restaurant and made our way back along the stunning pier. Earlier, there had been almost no people on the pier, but I was suddenly surprised to see a small group of people heading towards us. Douglas was a little ahead of me and suddenly began to say, in a partially hushed but rather excited tone, "It's Esther."

I looked with curiosity at the lady wearing big glasses, who was now in front of me, wondering if it could be. Douglas had had a misguided moment a few days ago when he thought she was getting into the same elevator as us; lol! Only this time, as soon as I heard her voice, I knew it really was Esther.

As if on cue and in reflection of our energetic openness, she joyfully asked us if we wanted a photo. We begin assembling together. Douglas passed his camera to Esther's photographer, who effortlessly took care of the photographic duties in a way that left Doug relieved and soon able to join us. It was all being taken care of so effortlessly and simply happening through us. Meanwhile, I'm standing with Esther in a delicious space; the energy is moving really fast. I'm enjoying the shared embrace and the natural connection present. And I'm feeling thrilled with this full, physical, sublime manifestation that I intended and allowed into being. Every component of this coming together this way was just divinely perfect.

—Izabella Siodmak

"Be thankful for what you have, you'll end up having more. If you concentrate on what you don't have, you will never have enough."
—*Oprah Winfrey*

Finding Money: What You Focus On

A while ago, I worked at a bakery. Each morning while it was still dark, I would set up tables and chairs outside, sweep the footpath, and put out signs.

One morning, I found a fifty-cent piece and picked it up. I smiled and thanked the universe for my morning tip. A few days later, I picked up a two-dollar coin, and after that, it became a regular occurrence. I was picking up coins of different denominations each time.

One day, it had been raining, and I looked around and asked jokingly, "Where is my tip for this morning?" Then I was drawn to look farther down the footpath, and up against a building, there was a twenty-dollar note. I was very excited and very appreciative. A few weeks later, I went outside the bakery, and lying on the ground was a fifty-dollar note. This all happened very early, and there was no one else anywhere to be seen at that time of the morning.

I fell into the habit of expecting the money to be there; I was focused on finding money. There was no resistance, and my mood was always light-hearted, fun, and appreciative, so I kept attracting more of that, and the more I appreciated even the small amounts, the greater the amounts I received.

There have been many times that I needed money but was unable to attract it because when I am in a state of needing the money, my awareness is much more on the lack of money, and so I attract that same result: a lack of money.

What we focus on, we create more of.

—Judi Mason

"You have brains in your head. You have feet in your shoes. You can steer yourself any direction you choose. You're on your own. And you know what you know. And YOU are the one who'll decide where to go..."
—Dr Seuss, Oh, The Places You Will Go.

A Trip to Paris

My eldest daughter, Christine, was going on a business trip. She was going to Kiev first, meeting up with a colleague, and then to Paris for five days. A few days before the trip, she was told her colleague would not be going to Paris. However, all accommodation and meals had already been paid for. Christine asked if I would like to go. I wanted to go, the desire was really strong, but I still had to come up with the airfare, and I did not have the money in the bank at that time.

My husband and I went to visit Christine on Saturday, as Sunday was both Mother's Day and the day she was flying out to Kiev. We sat around, having a few drinks and trying to brainstorm ways to get the money for me to join her. It was all in fun, and the more drinks we had, the more outrageous the suggestions. However, during the night, I suddenly remembered a trading account I had set up a while ago and had forgotten about, and although I wasn't actively trading, I knew there was still some money in the account. When I checked the account, there was, in fact, the exact amount of money I needed to fly to Paris. It was all set; I booked my airfare for the Thursday to arrive in Paris on Friday, the same day Christine would arrive from Kiev.

We had a fantastic time together. I loved Paris, and everything was paid for. From the moment I put the desire out there, everything just flowed to create the reality. I know that if I hadn't opened my mind to different possibilities, if I had just stated, "No, I don't have the money," the means would not have been revealed.

—Judi Mason

"One of the great cosmic laws, I think, is that whatever we hold in our thought will come true in our experience. When we hold something, anything, in our thought, then somehow coincidence leads us in the direction that we've been wishing to lead ourselves."

— *Richard Bach*

Unexplained Coincidence or ...?

I have a smart phone, which I love, although occasionally, I somehow accidentally initiate calls when the phone is in my pocket. This can be in my jeans pocket, my coat, or even on a few occasions the inside pocket of my suit jacket. Sometimes, I would hear the person talking from my pocket and get the phone out and say hello. Other times, I wouldn't hear it at all and only realised later, when I noticed the number on my call history. Generally, the calls were to either someone near the top of my phone directory or from the recent calls list.

On the occasion of one particular accidental call, I had been thinking about calling this person, let's call him Fred Smith, about a business opportunity. I couldn't find him in the recent call list, and he's not near the top of my alphabetic phone directory. In fact, I realised I hadn't spoken to him for about two years. It was only the fact that a business opportunity had been mentioned to me a few weeks earlier that made me think of him. And then I checked my phone, and there was his name. I had accidentally called him while the phone was in my pocket.

At this point, I thought, *What a funny coincidence.*

Later the same day, I was out to dinner with friends. We were discussing various projects and business opportunities, when one of my friends said, "Have you talked to Fred Smith? I haven't seen him for years."

At that point, I showed them my recent call list and said, "I haven't seen him for years either, but apparently I called him today."

—Clint Johnson

*"What the mind of man can conceive
and believe, it can achieve."*
                                        —*Napoleon Hill*

Ask, and You Will Receive

My son Josh wrote this on August 12, 2015:

"I will receive $5,000 extra cash by September 1, 2015 and cash comes freely and frequently for the rest of my life. I can buy everything my heart desires, and I am comfortably able to pay all of my bills."

He had been told by his employer that everyone would be getting a pay cut; the following is the text he sent to me on September 1, 2015:

"I wrote this earlier last month and had been focusing on it constantly, every time I feel really happy, I think of the $5,000. Today I received a phone call from my employer saying that it had been decided that I would no longer be receiving a pay cut! The date is September 1, 2015; the pay rate change is worth at least another $7,000 in my hand per year. I call that a very successful manifestation.

"Now to set my sights higher!"

I was very inspired by this and thought, *I'm going to do this.* However, I struggled with what amount to put down because I didn't want to put in an amount that was too high or too low, and I was not sure what date to put down because I didn't want to limit the time frame; it was really interesting to see where I was still focused on lack or fear.

Then I just said, "I am just going to copy what Josh had written." I wrote, "I will receive an extra $5,000 by the first of October, 2015." Then I completely forgot all about it.

On October 1, 2015, I sat down to sort out all of my paperwork and came across the piece of paper that I had written the above statement on. My first thought was, *Well, that's not going to happen now,* but I quickly reminded myself that there was still time; I had until midnight. Later that afternoon, I received a phone call, letting me know that we had a new tenant moving into one of our properties that had been vacant for over six months. I felt very happy, but it wasn't till later that I realised that the rent from that property would be worth another $8,000 per year.

When Josh shared his story with me, he inspired me to do the same, but he also showed me that there are many ways that the universe can deliver. Previously, if I asked for money, I would expect a lump sum of money, and sometimes it does happen that way, but in both these stories, the money came in different forms but on the exact day that had been written down.

Although both results are the same, Josh was able to keep focusing and feeling happy about it. For me, I had written it and forgotten all about it, but that worked for me because I would have been looking for it and fearing that it wouldn't be successful, so I would have probably blocked it.

—Judi Mason

Clothes

I had uncluttered my wardrobe and really needed to get some jeans and tops. In this small town, there was nothing suitable, and a trip away was a long way off. My neighbour had bought a few clothes for her daughter and then found that she had excess. She wondered if I would like to try them. Perfect fit and my style, and she would not accept any payment, so we shared a quiet wine that evening.

New Clothes

I was shopping with my daughter, and she was looking for a particular style of shorts. We found the style she wanted. However, there were none in her size on the rack. Close by, there was another similar style. Her size was available in this style, so she picked them up to try on. Suddenly, she put them back and said, "No, I won't try these. I will have the style I want. Someone has moved mine, and they will just come to me." Sure enough, a few aisles away, a pair of shorts had been left on top of a rack, her size, her style, and a perfect fit.

—Patti Henderson

What to Wear

One day recently, I walked into my bedroom to pack for a trip, and I said aloud to myself, "I need new jeans." I then opened my drawer to get my old jeans out, a drawer I use all of the time, and there under my old jeans was a brand-new pair of jeans, still with the tags on them. I don't remember buying them, and if I did, it would have been several months before because I hadn't been clothes shopping for ages. Wouldn't you think I would have seen them sitting there?

I was very happy and grateful for my brand-new pair of jeans manifesting exactly when I needed them. Thank you, universe.

—Judi Mason

Boots

I have been doing a lot of gardening lately, and every time I walked into the garden to weed or pick vegetables, my shoes got very muddy. I was watching a gardening video, and the woman was wearing gumboots, and I thought, *That's what I need.* I live in a very tiny town with very few shops and no clothes or shoe shops, so I looked online to see if I could order some, but I was surprised at the price of them and just put it aside for the time being. About a week later, I visited our local op shop, and there, sitting on the table as I walked in, was a pair of really good quality gumboots in my size. Thank you again, universe.

—Judi Mason

Something Shiny and Sparkly

My husband and I were camping at a dam site where the water levels were quite low, and we were walking along the edge of the dam. This was an old gold mining area, and a lot of people go out there fossicking. As we walked along, I said jokingly, "Keep your eyes out for anything shiny and sparkly."

Greg immediately picked up an old bottle top and asked, "Like this?"

I smiled, but just a bit farther along, I saw a ring, and as I picked it up, I said, "No, like this." I thought it was a child's toy ring at first, but when I picked it up, it looked like a real gold ring with sapphires in it.

I asked at the office if anyone had lost it, but no one had reported it.

I was half-joking when I said it but thought it would be fun to find gold. Being in a pleasant, relaxed state and having no resistance to receiving allowed me to find exactly what I had asked for, something shiny and sparkly.

—Judi Mason

Manifesting a Real Diamond

My name is Al Faustino, but my friends call me Namaste. I live in Las Vegas, Nevada, and have a day job doing merchandising at the Las Vegas airport. In late 2009, I was at the airport when I ran into a janitor I knew. I don't remember exactly how, but we ended up talking about all the things he had found over the years at the airport. In passing, he mentioned that another janitor found a $10,000 Rolex watch a short time ago. She was walking into the airport when a glint caught her eye from something next to the curb. She couldn't tell what it was because of the way the sun was hitting it, so she walked over to investigate. To her surprise, when she reached the curb, she picked up a solid gold Rolex watch with a diamond dial. Luckily for the man who lost it, she turned it into lost and found. A man called a few days later; it slipped out of his pocket when he was getting into a limousine, which explained how it ended up against the curb. It was this passing comment about finding a Rolex that had a huge impact on me a few months later.

In February of 2010, I proposed to my girlfriend, and she said yes. I was in the middle of launching a new business at the time, and money was tight. I wanted to get her a beautiful ring, but I was short on funds. I racked my brain, thinking about every way I could get her the kind of ring I wanted. I thought about going to a pawnshop, but I didn't like the idea of buying a ring that had been pawned. Then

127

I thought about financing a ring and paying it off over time, but I didn't like that either. Next, I found a national park online called Crater of Diamonds, a state park in Arkansas. You can go there, and for a small fee, you get to dig for diamonds. Sometimes, people find really nice ones. However, I found out the park is only open during the summer, and I didn't want to wait that long. Finally, I remembered the story of the janitor finding the Rolex. I thought to myself, *If a janitor can find a $10,000 Rolex watch, I bet I can manifest myself finding a diamond ring at the airport.* I thought about this for a while and decided it was my best option.

A few days later, I was once again walking around the airport, and I realised I had a problem. If I found a diamond ring and turned it into lost and found, there was a good chance the person who lost it would claim it before the thirty days was up (after which time, if nobody claimed it, it would be turned over to me). Plus I realised I *really* didn't like the thought of giving my new bride-to-be someone else's wedding ring. It just felt wrong, and I'd feel bad for the person who lost it.

This stumped me for a while until I realised that I could manifest just finding a diamond without the ring. I had no idea how this was possible, but it was the only way I felt comfortable, so that's what I went with. I put my request out to the universe to find a diamond and promptly forgot about it.

One day a few months later, I arrived at the airport and clocked in. As I was walking out of the store, I looked down and saw a gemstone. It was bigger than the ones I normally saw, so I picked it and turned it over in my hand. Fake gemstones were always falling off of people's clothing, purses, and fake jewellery, so it was pretty routine for me to see them at the airport. I was just about to throw it away when I realised something odd. The stone had inclusions in it. I'd learned when I was researching diamonds that most diamonds have little cracks in them that are called inclusions (unless, of course, the diamond is flawless, which was extremely expensive and incredibly rare). The diamond was so big; it couldn't be real, but just in case, I kept it.

What's funny is, at the time, I wasn't excited. I guess that was probably because it was so big that I didn't see how it could be real. A few days later, I told my fiancée about what I'd found, and we decided to go to a jewellery store on our day off. As we were driving to the store, I felt a twinge of excitement. What if it was real? It seemed impossible, being that big, but I'd wanted a big stone; what if it really was a genuine diamond?

We drove to a jewellery store in North Las Vegas and went in. We were greeted by a clerk, and I told her my story.

She said, "Well, let's test it."

I handed her the stone, and she went and got a handheld gadget. She placed the diamond in it and pulled the trigger; the light on the side went red, and she said, "Congratulations; you found a real diamond."

I was stunned; it just seemed so hard to believe. I'd manifested lots of things before, but never anything this valuable.

I asked her, "How is it possible that I found this diamond? Did a jeweller lose it or something?"

She said, "No, the prongs on a ring that holds the centre stone in place wear down over time as a person bumps it into stuff in their daily life. If the ring isn't checked, eventually one of the prongs wears down, and the stone falls out. This is why we tell people to come in once a year and have their rings cleaned and checked."

As I walked out of the jewellery store that day, my mind was reeling. I thought, *If it's possible to manifest a diamond, it's possible to manifest anything.*

—Al Faustino

COYO

Editor's note: *Henry has always been one to want to try something new in business. His background was in media: running, restructuring, or creating newspapers. He along with his wife, Sandra, ran a café, created a vegetable processing and salad business, and managed a cheese factory.*

Henry was born in Fiji and is no stranger to the coconut. He spent his school holidays on friends' coconut plantations in Savu Savu, which is on the main island of Vanua Levu. Here he learnt how to collect, husk, cut, and remove the whole flesh of the coconut.

He and Sandra took the knowledge they have of the coconut and created COYO, a company specialising in coconut products.

What a Journey This has Been
It all started in August 2009, when I was looking at coconut oil with the view to exporting it to Israel. I met with Ken Sigrah and Stacey King, who owned Nature Pacific. They asked me if I could make coconut butter, as they knew that I had been the general manager of Kenilworth Country Foods, known as the Cheese Factory. I replied that I could not but would give it some thought.

They say that if you put an idea out in the universe, that somewhere, sometime, something will come back to you. I had heard of the law of attraction and *The Secret* but had not taken it too seriously.

Three weeks after my visit, I woke up on a Sunday morning. "I've had this idea," I said as Sandra stirred. "What is it this time?" she asked. "What time is it?" "2 a.m., and I am going to check this idea out." "What is it?"

"Yoghurt made from coconut milk."

"You have got to be crazy," she said, adding before she went back to sleep, "Henry, I hope this is not another one of your ideas that will send us broke."

I got onto the computer and typed in "coconut milk yoghurt," and within a few minutes, the screen came up with a lot of forums. I searched for companies that made the yoghurt, but there was none except a company called Turtle Mountain. They were in Oregon in the United States.

Sandra wandered into the office a few hours later. "What are you doing?" she asked.

"I am looking for coconut milk yoghurt manufacturers," I said.

"Where did you get this crazy idea from?" she asked.

"Remember my visit to Nature Pacific? Well, it's the law of attraction. I have been thinking about coconuts, and this is what has come up from out there," I replied, pointing out the window into the universe.

"But Henry, you've never made yoghurt."

"I know, but let's see where this takes us."

The Experiments Begin

Making yoghurt from scratch is not easy. After scanning the forums online, I printed out just about every recipe there was. I tracked scientific papers from the university in Ghana to just about every piece of information on yoghurt that was known to humankind, but alas, there was no commercial coconut milk yoghurt recipes or companies. I joined the online community and then started what was to become a long journey.

Our kitchen started to look like a war zone. Every day, I made a batch of yoghurt, then two batches, then four batches, then six batches a day. I made different recipes every day, and then I would throw them out. After a month, Sandra was getting agitated. She could not get into the kitchen before midday as I made, searched, and searched again for the right way.

After a month, I got hold of Barry Lillywhite from Wagga Wagga. I needed to get some real cultures rather than using yoghurts from the supermarket. Barry was in charge of a cheese-making facility at Wagga Wagga and listened to my story. He offered to send me samples of various cultures. It was now starting to get very serious. I went back to the batches with the real stuff, and reported the progress to Barry, but still no success. It was all becoming frustrating; my short fuse was now so much shorter, as I just could not get it to work.

I rang Barry. "Gee, Henry," he said, "you are really keen on this."

Keen? It had now become an obsession. What's more, I now had Sandra involved. She understood it all. She had read Dr Bruce Fife's excellent book, *The Miracle of the Coconut*, and just was blown away by the information about the coconut. I read the book, and after all these years of living in Fiji, I do not think any of us had any understanding of what this nut had in it.

"Henry," Barry said, "you live in Fiji and must have known about the health benefits of the coconut."

"No," I replied, "we just had coconut every day, and it was just part of the diet; no one mentioned health benefits to any of us."

The more we researched about the coconut, the more doors seemed to open. People were so generous with their ideas and suggestions to us. It was like out there in the universe, someone was looking down on us, passing us information and telling people to contact us.

This new information just added fuel to an already overheated motor.

Barry sent more information on each culture and then suggested a couple he thought of in the middle of the night. He was getting into the law of attraction as well.

On November 17, 2009, I made a batch, and when I looked at it the next day, I brought the container to Sandra.

"Oh no, not another one," she said.

She was still in bed; it was early morning, and tears were just rolling down my face.

"I've done it," I said. "We have made yoghurt from coconut milk."

Sandra jumped out of bed, put the spoon in the container, tasted it, and hugged me.

"What's in it?" she asked.

"That, my dear, is our little secret."

Now we had yoghurt, but where and how were we going to convert a kitchen experiment into a commercial operation?

More importantly, did we have a market?

I made up more batches, and Sandra took them to her yoga classes each week. Yes, the response was fabulous; they loved it.

We *did* have a market, and what's more, one lady said that it tasted like "heaven in a mouthful."

Sandra had always asked me about where we would get the yoghurt made. My response was always to see if we could make it first, but now we had to get it to the commercial level.

Naming the Product

About the same time, Jackie and Philip, friends from New Zealand, arrived to stay a few weeks with us. They had been friends for years.

"So what are you going to call it?" they asked.

We tossed about a few ideas, and then Jackie said, "What about COYO?"

"Nice ring about it," said Sandra.

Yes, COYO did sound good. Within a day, the name was registered, and the yoghurt that had taken so long to develop finally had a name: COYO.

From Theory to Reality

When I was the general manager at Kenilworth Cheese Factory, Dick Schroder was a farmer who supplied us with milk and cream now and then. Dick owned Cooloola Milk. He was the first Queenslander to milk his cows and then bottle the milk on-site.

I heard that Dick had a yoghurt plant at his factory in Dagun and went to see him. We talked about the plant, and I went and had a look at the factory.

I went home and talked to Sandra about it, and we decided that we should make a batch and take it out to Dick for him to try.

Sandra and I called on Dick again; and after a lot of argy-bargy, he finally agreed that I could make the yoghurt at the plant.

"But Henry, I am not making it," he said. "You must be crazy to want to make yoghurt, but that's your business."

I pulled out the sample. Dick tried it; he looked at us and then took another spoon full, then another.

"Looks like a winner to me, Henry."

As Sandra and I drove home, she said to me, "Henry, you have never made yoghurt; we must be mad."

Crunch Time

We had come all this way, the frustration and inconvenience of having the kitchen out of action for six months, and now it was crunch time. I suggested that we make a small batch, and Sandra thought we should have a reasonable size one. Our research showed that there was a market, and 250 kilograms would be a good starter. On make day, Sandra suggested we go for 500 kilograms.

I drove to the factory, where I met Jarred, who worked for Dick and had made yoghurt for the Queensland Yoghurt Company. Jarred was to show me how to work the equipment.

I told Jarred that this was no ordinary yoghurt and it was to be made out of coconut milk. He looked at me, and I could tell that he had to rethink his whole idea on making yoghurts, especially as I said we would be skipping some of the conventional methods in the production cycle.

Unbeknown to me, Jarred also had a partner who was due to have a baby that day. The batch was made in between text messages between Jarred and his partner.

We set the yoghurt, and Jarred left to check on his partner. He gave me instructions on what to do, what tap to turn this way or that.

I looked around at the place and wondered what could possibly go wrong.

When it came to getting the yoghurt out of the tank, I had it all organised. Nothing to it, just start the pump and open the taps. The taps were open, the pump was on, and the yoghurt started to flow.

I knew from Kenilworth days that the first couple of buckets were always runny, as it was the yoghurt in the pipes flowing, not the product from the tank. It flowed out, and it was runny. This was normal, I thought. But it wasn't just two buckets; it was bucket, after bucket.

I thought to myself, *All this time, effort, testing, retesting and now this.* I sent a silent plea to the universe: *Where are you? Whoever you are out there, what has happened? I need you now.*

I could not believe what I was seeing. I emptied bucket after bucket of runny yoghurt.

What would Sandra think? We had a lot at stake here. How could I face her with this news?

I stopped the pump and looked into the tank. It all looked okay, but something was wrong. The timing was right; mentally I redid the calculations from the one-litre test to a five-hundred-litre make. I turned the pump on again and watched it pour out. Twelve, thirteen, fourteen buckets, and then I wondered whether I should just open the taps and let it go down the drain, go home, and face whatever was going to be.

We had a lot of money invested in this venture, and here I was, at the factory looking at disaster. Buckets fifteen, sixteen, seventeen. I was ready to call it quits. Almost. But as I looked at the yoghurt again, it started to change. It was becoming thicker. I looked again at bucket eighteen, and it was as if I was back at Kenilworth. The yoghurt looked good, bloody good. I could not believe that we had finally created yoghurt made from coconut milk.

My eyes just opened, and tears of joy fell from them, streaming down my face as I bucketed the remaining thirty-three buckets.

The mobile phone rang.

"Hi, it's me. I have not heard from you."

"The winner is Sydney," I yelled down the phone. Sandra knew what that meant. (That's what they said when Sydney was selected for the Olympics.)

"You are not kidding, are you, Henry?"

"The winner is Sydney," I said again.

"Oh my God, bring some home, won't you?"

Jarred arrived back, reporting that there was still no action on the baby front at home. I shook his hand and congratulated him on contributing to the making of the first coconut yoghurt in Australia.

When I arrived home, Sandra rushed out to greet me. "Let me have a look," she said.

I opened the bucket and cautioned her that we needed to wait until morning for the real test of how successful we had been, but it was looking good.

In the morning, I got up and went to the fridge, opened the bucket, and there it was.

Sandra and I had created the first commercial batch of coconut yoghurt in Australia.

The rest, as they say, is history.

COYO has now become the brand name for all our coconut products. Our Coconut Milk Yoghurt has now been refined to be dairy free, gluten free, soy free, lactose free, and sweetened with Xylitol, not sucrose. We also launched our Coconut Milk Ice Cream.

Colin Cunningham from Colin James Fine Foods makes it for us, and it is just so delicious. We are also the distributors for Pearl Royal, in my view the best coconut water on the market today. In my mind, this journey has been a combination of perseverance and the law of attraction working together.

—Henry Gosling

(**Editor's note:** Henry asked and was open to receive; in the middle of the night, he received the idea, and because of Henry's and Sandra's trust and willingness to follow through, the universe delivered so many people to help. They never gave up and now have an incredible, unique, delicious, and healthy product for us all to enjoy. Thank you, Henry and Sandra.—JM)

Part 2

The Bad

Maybe It's Bad; Maybe It Isn't. Who Knows?

*"There is nothing either good or
bad, but thinking makes it so."*
—William Shakespeare, Hamlet

*"There is not something you're supposed to
do. There's not something that you should do.
There is only that which you are inspired to
do. And how do you get inspired except by
the contrast? It's the life experience that gives
you the idea of the desire, and then as you
focus upon the desire, the Energy flows."*
—Abraham

*Excerpted from the workshop in
Philadelphia on Tuesday, April 14, 1998.*[i]

Appreciating the Contrast

Sometimes, things seem to go wrong or seem to be a bit of a challenge. Contrast shows us what we don't want and is often the catalyst to propel us towards what we do want in our lives. It is at these times when we really appreciate the contrast; for example, when we're feeling unwell, we really appreciate health.

One day, when we were driving on an unfamiliar highway, we became aware very quickly how bad this road was. Parts of it were dirt, and they were the good parts; the rest was so rough, we felt like we were being shaken up. I joked that the eggs in the car would now be scrambled. Then we reached a new part of the road, and it was so smooth. We really appreciated the contrast. However, we drive on good roads most of the time, and we take it for granted; it is only the contrast that makes us appreciate the opposite and know more clearly what it is we really do want.

When I look back over the year that was, there have been many challenging moments, weeks, and months, as there have been for many people in many different circumstances. However, it has also been an incredible year in many, many ways. This year, we went on a cruise around Tahiti, and not long after arriving home, we were told we were going on another cruise, all paid for with our mentoring group. We have spent a lot of time with the most amazing, inspiring group of people who we had the good fortune to meet up with every two months throughout the year and who we have become great friends with. We are continually learning and growing and noticing the contrasts and, because of the contrast, expanding and appreciating our life even more.

—Judi Mason

"The law of attraction attracts to you everything you need, according to the nature of your thought life. Your environment and your financial condition are the perfect reflection of your habitual thinking. Thought rules the world."

—Joseph Murphy

The Flower Brooch

This is a story about energy in action. My daughter Rebecca was visiting me with her husband and their three children. The youngest, Chelsea, who was three months old at the time, was wearing a beautiful little dress with a colourful flower brooch attached to it. After a while, one of us noticed that the brooch was missing. Rebecca was very upset and put a lot of energy into searching for the brooch, then a lot more energy into being upset about losing the brooch. She was sure it was lost forever.

A little while later, we went out to the local markets, and while looking through her bag for something else, Rebecca found the brooch. She had looked in the bag thoroughly before that and so was surprised, and pleased, to find it there. She pinned the brooch to the dress, and we continued walking around the market stalls. A short time later, she looked down, and the brooch was gone. Rebecca *knew* that because of the energy she had put into being upset about the brooch being lost, she had now *created* the brooch being lost. Our husbands both backtracked to where we had been but could not find the brooch. I suggested that now she should focus on being happy about finding it and keep that vibration going.

I had the urge to go back to one particular stall (out of hundreds of stalls) and ask them if they had seen the brooch. They said they had not but did remember seeing it on the dress at the time. They suggested that I go to the office and put my name down so that if it was handed to any of the stallholders, I could claim it. I was disappointed because I had been sure that I would find it, but I stayed optimistic that it would turn up eventually. When I caught up with everybody, Rebecca looked on the ground and for a split-second thought that she had found the brooch, but on the ground was a cardboard flower, similar in size and colour to the brooch. I said that it was a sign and picked it up and sat it in Chelsea's pram. Later on that day, we received a phone call from the stallholder I had spoken to. She had found the brooch.

Rebecca was so happy, but as they had to leave for the drive home, over six hours away, the stallholder said she would post the brooch. Once again, Rebecca was happy and grateful. A few days later, a parcel arrived with the brooch and a gift of a beautiful new dress for Chelsea.

—Judi Mason

Time to Read

I had an acquaintance once who was busy working all of the time. She would complain and say, "I would just love to have time to lay in bed all day and read books." Shortly after this, she broke her leg, and guess what? All she could do was lay in bed all day and read books.

—Judi Mason

At My Worst

When I was twenty-one, I was going through the most challenging period of my life. I was quite negative, and as a result, everything seemed to be going from bad to worse. I found myself complaining all the time and saying, "Give me a break; give me a break." Well, within two weeks of saying this over and over, I finally *did* get my break, in the form of a broken toe. Ask, and you shall receive; just be careful what you ask for. I've never said that again and have never had a break since.

—Rachael Bermingham

Be Careful What You Wish For

I'd been invited to a business event in the United States. The local account manager would accompany my manager and me on the trip, acting as the chaperone/organiser. All sounds great so far, although I have to tell you that the account manager is an incessant talker and very intense about all things related to her company.

In discussing this with my manager, he said, "Well, you're going to have to sit with her on the plane," and my response was, "No, you do; you're the senior person she needs to convince to win our business." This discussion continued for many weeks prior the departure. It became a bit of a standing joke between our peers and us.

On the day of our departure, we all met at Melbourne airport for a connecting flight to Sydney and then on to San Francisco. At Melbourne, we were checked in for both legs of the journey. The three of us checked in separately, so when we met up, there was still some mystery around who would be sitting with whom.

My manager was still muttering to me as we boarded the plane to Sydney, "If I'm next to her, you're going to have to swap."

This was, of course, all in jest, and as it turned out, we were all sitting separately on the first leg anyway.

We made it to Sydney and were waiting in the domestic-to-international transfer lounge, when our account manager announced, "I haven't got my passport."

At first, I thought she was joking but then witnessed the contents of her handbag being emptied onto the seats. The assistant at the Melbourne check-in had failed to return her passport, and until this point in time, she hadn't realised. Of course, no passport means you cannot pass through customs, and so you cannot travel internationally. Thus my manager and I departed without our chaperone. Over the two months or so before my trip, I had shared the banter about seating arrangements for the flight with my wife, and she warned me to be careful what you wish for. Now, reflecting on my wife's words of wisdom, and witnessing the stress the poor account manager was going through, I thought to myself, *I'm never going to do that sort of thing again, even if it means sitting for fourteen hours next to someone I'd prefer not to.*

Fortunately, the airport staff delivered her passport to her by the end of the day. The following morning, she was able to catch a flight to LA then to San Francisco, just in time for our first presentation of the trip. Once we all caught up in San Francisco, we enjoyed our trip, including several social evenings for dinner and drinks. This gave us all a chance to get to know each other a bit better.

On the return trip, we checked in together, and wouldn't you know it? I was sitting next to her for the flight from LA to Melbourne. She must have sensed the earlier sentiments and asked if I wanted her to swap seats.

I said, "No, don't be silly; it's fine."

At the time, I was thinking to myself that for most of the trip, we'd be watching movies with our headsets on or be asleep, anyway.

Whether the universe was involved or not, my video screen wasn't working. The flight attendant apologised but said all business class seats were allocated, so he couldn't do much about it.

The irony of this is, we got to know each other very well on the flight home, and although I don't deal with this person on a business level anymore, we stay in contact. I could so easily have missed out on the opportunity to get to know another person, simply because of my preconceptions.

—Clint Johnson

Lessons Learnt

Five years ago, I hadn't even heard of the law of attraction, and I thought spirituality was for the hippies. At this time in my life, I was feeling pretty good: I had a good marriage, great kids, and just renovated my home, and financially, we were comfortable. Then it all changed. My marriage ended, my children were shattered, and I had to sell our home.

At the time of my deepest despair, I was introduced to Soraya, a reiki master, naturopath, and spiritual healer. She reached out to me, and through her support, encouragement, and love, I began my own healing process and in time became a reiki master and spiritual teacher, sharing my healing journey with others and assisting others through their healing journey.

This is my story of how I began my spiritual journey and discovered the truth about the law of attraction.

"Go to Vanuatu and open a spiritual centre." The voice in my head was really clear. So I did.

I sold my family home and our car, put all our possessions in storage, packed up my two children, aged seven and ten, and with just a suitcase each, we headed off to a country we had never seen. We knew no one, had no home to go to and no job to go to, and had no idea what we were going to do next. I promised myself and my family that I would be home in a few months if we didn't settle there.

Once we arrived, we fell in love with the place, the people, and the energy of the islands. I was so focused and determined on making sure this venture worked that for the first time in my life, I decided to hand it over to the universe and test if this spiritual stuff really worked.

It seemed that we were going to be tested by the universe. Within the first two weeks, my youngest child suffered from incredibly painful and infected wounds on her legs, and I had eye infections that were painful, were ugly, and temporarily made me lose my vision. Here we were, in a third-world country with no real medical treatment available and all alone. What had I done? I felt real fear at this and wondered if it were a test to send us packing and Australia bound.

So I asked the universe to show me what to do; do I return to the familiarity and comfort of Australia or stay in Vanuatu to follow my spiritual path? That very day, someone told me about an Australian doctor travelling through Vila, and we were able to see him and receive some good medical care. Lesson one learned.

For the first time in my life, I actually felt lonely, so I asked the universe to bring me some friends and contacts who would help me create my business.

The next day, I had just crossed the road when I heard that voice in my head say, "Turn around now." I did, and that action alone caught the attention of a lady about to cross the road right in front of a bus. In Vanuatu, cars drive on the right-hand side of the road, and she had looked the other way. We often said that the action of me turning around had saved her life.

This lady had lived only an hour away from me in Australia and now became my first friend in Vila. We soon discovered many similarities between us, one of which was her desire to start a spiritual centre. We became business partners and created Lotus Health and Beauty, a six-room day spa and spiritual centre with yoga, reiki, reflexology, and various spiritual workshops. Lesson two learned.

There was a time during the building of this business that I began to fear not having enough money. It became all I could think about. Budgeting was hard, as with most small businesses, the income was less than the outgoings. I had bills to pay, staff to pay, licences to pay for; the list went on and on. By now, I had begun to realise the power of "What you think, you will create," but do you think I could get away from that fearful voice in my head and the reality I was living?

I was about to get a big lesson in the power of our thoughts.

I withdrew a large sum of money and went to work, became sidetracked, and forgot about the money until the next morning. Overnight, I left my handbag in my bedroom beside my bed, and in the morning, to my shock, I discovered the money was missing. Had someone stolen it from inside my locked home, while I was asleep? Was I the victim of what the locals refer to as black magic? Had it been stolen by one of my staff or a contractor the previous day at my office? I felt so mean having these accusing thoughts but didn't know what else to think.

I was upset but knew there was little to be done about it. The next day, I withdrew the same amount of money again and this time came straight home with it and left it on the kitchen counter overnight. In the morning, I followed the usual routine of opening up windows, waking kids up, showering, making lunches, and left the kitchen for a few minutes, only to return to find the money missing again.

Now there was only myself and my two children home, so I wondered if something had happened that one of my children needed the money; were they being bullied? I hated accusing them, but with little evidence to go on, I didn't know what to make of it. They tearfully told me it wasn't them, and they were so sad to be blamed like this. I actually left a jar out in the bathroom and suggested that if someone in the house had the missing money, they could replace it no questions asked.

Days went by, and the money was not returned. I let it out of my mind, and then I noticed a cut fly screen in the kitchen. It now appeared that someone must have climbed in when I had left the kitchen for those few minutes and taken the money from the bench. Boy, that was fast.

That week was Independence Week in Vila, one of the biggest celebrations held each year. There were parties and celebrations and festivals and visitors from all the outer islands. The quiet streets of Vanuatu, where everyone knew you, were transformed into a carnival city full of strangers. Over the weekend, numbers increased as did levels of kava and alcohol consumption.

It had been my son's birthday that day, and he had some mates sleeping over, so I left them watching TV and went to bed early. I was woken a couple of hours later by that voice in my head again, yelling, "Wake up now!" I opened my eyes to see a young islander man in my bedroom, shining a torch into the cupboard, where my handbag was. I was so shocked that I didn't have time to feel frightened. I just wanted him out of my home.

I yelled at him, "Get out! Get out of my house!" I chased him through the house but didn't see if he got out or was still inside the house.

I stood in the hallway with my heart thumping in my chest, not knowing where any of the children in my house were, if they were safe, or where the intruder was. I began yelling the children's names and asking them to answer me and tell me where they were, asking them if they were safe. Thankfully, they had slept through it all and were only cranky at being woken in the middle of the night by my yelling.

I noticed that a row of louvres had been removed from the lounge room where I had last seen the intruder and realised that he must have jumped through them. That didn't mean that my legs weren't shaking when I had to go and check all the rooms, just in case. When I checked my purse in the bedroom cupboard, the money had gone with him.

Now, where were my thoughts that week? Honestly, my thoughts were fearful, concerned with losing money in my business and not having enough money to survive. In response to that fear, I had created an experience where someone who had a stronger fear of not having enough money was desperate enough to rob me three times in the one week. Boy, did he get lucky with this naive Aussie girl. I certainly experienced the law of attraction in its negative form that week. Another lesson learned.

My landlord and local community were outraged that we had endured this frightening experience. I had many offers for extra security at night and was gifted a four-legged guard, a German shepherd watchdog, the fabulous Shadow. After a week of security patrolling the house and sleeping on the deck, the dog and my two children sharing my bedroom, and the house and yard lit up like a Christmas tree, I knew we had to let go of the fear and get back to normal. We bravely said goodbye to our extra staff, turned off the lights, and banished the children and the dog from my room. Life returned to normal, and I watched my thoughts very carefully from then on.

Two years later, I sold my share of the business and decided to return to Australia. Once again, I had nowhere to live, no car, and no job in sight. I asked the universe to provide the right home, car, and work for me. The week I was due to fly out, I checked my emails, and there was a message from an ex-neighbour in Caloundra, asking me if I wanted to rent their house by the beach, and a message from my nana, saying her sister had a car she wanted to sell me. I smiled and said thank you to the universe. I arrived home, and two days later, I had a place to live, a car to drive, and the beginning of a new business idea.

The law of attraction strikes again, positively.

Over the past three years, I have built a successful business upon practising and teaching how to tap into this universal energy through reiki and other energy healing modalities. I express these teachings further through reiki workshops and the Enlightened Goddesses Business Network by encouraging others to become aware of their thoughts and to take responsibility for their lives. By practising conscious awareness and having the belief that we can have, do, and be all that we want, we can work with the law of the universe to create great lives.

I now tap into this universal energy and use the law of attraction to create the experiences that I wish to have in my life. I make sure that I am consciously aware of the thoughts and beliefs that I hold to ensure that I only attract great experiences into my life. I teach my children and my clients how to use the law of attraction to create magic and to bring clarity, direction, and ease into their life.

Life was not meant to be hard. There is no one to blame when life does get hard for us. We need to take responsibility for our lives and the situations that we experience. When we consciously tap into and become connected to the universal energy that creates everything around us, then we can create from that same powerful space, and magic happens.

Our thoughts create our reality. What thoughts are creating your reality right now?

—Natalie McIvor

The Hill

When I was learning to drive, everyone talked about the dreaded hill start. This became embedded in my mind, and even though I actually had no trouble with hill starts when I was learning, it still gave me fear every time I had to do it.

Years went by, and I lived in many places with no hills, so there was no problem; however, we recently moved to an area where there were many hills, and one in particular really scared me. It was a very steep hill going up to a set of traffic lights on a very busy intersection, and every time I drove up this road, the fear set in. I dreaded having to use this road, and I always feared rolling back into the car behind me, and of course, I seemed to have to use this road more and more, and the cars always seemed to pull up very close behind me.

Because of this fear from thirty years ago, I would then panic and try to take off quickly, and I *always* stalled the vehicle. I then panicked even more and would start the car and plant my foot on the accelerator, and the car would squeal all the way through the intersection. I would be so embarrassed, and this made me dread that hill even more.

I recognised that my fear was creating this situation, so I decided to change my focus and visualise myself smoothly and slowly accelerating when the lights turned green and going through the intersection without stalling or squealing the tyres. Now I have no problems. I no longer fear that hill, and if the fear creeps in, I stop myself and again see myself driving through effortlessly. Since I have done this, it seems I hardly ever need to use this road anymore.

This is just another example of the power of our minds, for good and bad.

—Judi Mason

*"I attract to my life whatever I give
my attention, energy, and focus to,
whether positive or negative."*
—Michael Losier

Brakes Aren't the Only Things that Stop Us

We were having trouble with the brakes on our car, so Greg removed the brake booster to get it sent away to be reconditioned. He spoke to the workshop and was told it would only take a day. Great. On that same day (Wednesday), Greg also ordered a new master cylinder from a different company, one he had used several times previously, with a fast two-day turnaround every time.

Greg's vibrations began to slip when he received word that the transport company scheduled to take the brake booster to the workshop was delayed. Late in the afternoon the following day, the booster was picked up and on the way to the workshop, just three hours' drive from home. Phew.

Greg phoned the workshop on the Friday afternoon and was told they still hadn't received the brake booster. With no car, his frustrations were beginning to build. He then rang the transport company, but they didn't know where it was. Apparently, their computers were down, so they could not track it. On Saturday, he rang again; still no news on the whereabouts of the brake booster.

Greg was getting very angry about the situation and stated he could have walked the part to the workshop by now. There was a lot of energy focused on the part being lost. Eventually, the part did turn up at the workshop the following Tuesday morning, and it was repaired and sent straight back to us.

Then we realised the other part, the master cylinder, had not arrived, so Greg rang that company to find out where it was. Guess what? It was now missing. The company had not received it from their supplier; in fact, they didn't even realise until Greg rang them that there was a problem. So now, we were waiting for that part to turn up. The strange thing about that is you usually cannot order anything from their online store unless it is already in stock. Several days later, our master cylinder did turn up, and our car was back on the road again.

As I have mentioned in several stories, Greg is a powerful manifestor, and I have no doubt in my mind, because of the *negative* energy he had put into being angry about the missing part, he also manifested that the second part went missing.

—Judi Mason

Part 3

The Funny

"Our subconscious minds have no sense of humour, play no jokes and cannot tell the difference between reality and an imagined thought or image. What we continually think about eventually will manifest in our lives."

—Robert Collier

Spirit of Tasmania

I was living in Sydney, and for a long time, I wanted to go to Tasmania. To get to Tasmania, you cross the Bass Strait on a passenger and vehicle ferry, *The Spirit of Tasmania*, which departed from Melbourne. This is a huge ferry with cabins, dining rooms, and bars, like a cruise ship. One year, it was announced that the ferry was going to start departures from Sydney Harbour as well as from Melbourne.

I had heard about writing your goals and doing up vision boards, so I made a vision board, and on it, I put a picture of *The Spirit of Tasmania* and also wrote, "I am going on *The Spirit of Tasmania* at Sydney Harbour."

A short while later, I received an invitation to go onto the *Spirit of Tasmania* to have a tour of the ship while it was docked in Sydney Harbour. I really should have specified that I wanted to go to Tasmania on it.

—Paula Buchanan

DVD Player

We were heading off on a family holiday with our two sons. They were around four and seven years old at the time and a challenge to travel with. Our destination was over eight hours away, and I was trying to come up with something to keep them occupied in the car on this long drive.

What I really wanted was a DVD player for the car, but since we were about to go on holidays, I didn't want to spend too much on it. I thought it might be possible to rent one, so I called all around town to ask, but no one had any available. Then as I was on my way home, just around the corner from my house, I spotted something lying on the road. A portable DVD player. I jumped out to look at it. It was mangled and broken into pieces, but it was a DVD player. I guess I didn't specify that I wanted a *working* DVD player.

—Rebecca Malcomson

Getting Caught

It was a cold winter morning, and I had been lazing around in my pyjamas and feeling very warm and comfortable. I heard the mailman out the front, so I decided to sneak out to check my mail. I was worried someone would see me in my pyjamas at this late hour, so I looked out and, with no neighbours to be seen, I dashed towards the mailbox. At that moment, I heard a car coming along the road, so I quickly ran to our garage and hid inside, waiting for the car to pass, but the car kept coming. Then it slowed right down, and as I waited anxiously for it to pass, it turned into our driveway. I was forced to go and ask the driver what he wanted. I was feeling very embarrassed. After talking with the man, it turned out he had come to the wrong address; he was supposed to be on the next street over.

I know this is a silly little story, but it was also a huge lesson. I know that I was so focused on not wanting to be seen that I attracted not just someone glimpsing me in my pyjamas, but someone driving right in, forcing me to talk to them in my pyjamas.

—Judi Mason

Aussie Flag

It was coming up to Australia Day, and I was feeling very patriotic. My husband and I had gone to the bottle shop to get a couple of drinks, but I saw on the sign that if you spent over thirty dollars, you would receive an Aussie flag to attach to your car. I said he might as well get a few more drinks so I could have the flag. Obviously, he was quite happy to get a few more beers to make up the total. But when he came out he didn't have the flag.

So I asked my brother-in-law, who worked at a bottle shop, to get one for me next time he went to work. But he couldn't find them.

I was disappointed that I didn't have a flag to attach to my car, and as Australia Day approached, everywhere I went, people had car flags.

"I really want one," I said to my husband as we passed yet another car with flags, this one with *three* of them.

"How badly do you really want one?" he replied, pointing to the middle of the very busy highway.

There lying in the middle was a flag with the car attachment. I was too scared to run out on the road and get it, but it just goes to show that the universe always provides; sometimes, you just have to meet it halfway. Next time, I just hope it's not halfway across a very busy road.

—Rebecca Malcomson

My Car
(Getting What You Think You Don't Want)

I wanted a car, something small, easy to get around in, fairly new, and easy to afford. However, when my husband asked, "What sort of car do you want?" I said, "Well, I'll tell you what I *don't* want: I *don't* want a hatchback, and I *don't* want a silver car, and I *don't* want a manual car." I didn't tell him what I *did* want. This went on for a little while, with us both casually looking in car sales and on the internet. Then one day I made the decision that I wanted a car straight away and started to seriously look for a car.

That afternoon, Greg noticed a car on the side of the road for sale and came home to tell me about it. He said, "It looked like a nice car, but it was silver."

I said, "Let's look at it anyway."

We drove there, and it was silver, it was a manual, and it was a hatchback. But it was also small, easy to drive, nearly brand new (only eight thousand kilometres on the odometer, and still under warranty), and easy to afford. The owner was very reluctant to part with it but was moving back to England and had to sell it straight away. I loved it, and we were able to go and get the cash out of the bank that afternoon and drive it home.

I think it's funny that I got exactly what I was focused on *not* getting, but also that the universe found me a car that was perfect for me, even though I didn't know what really I wanted. I love my car, and I am grateful every day for it.

—Judi Mason

Sold

We owned a house that we had renovated just down the road from where we live, and it was on the market. Every day my husband, Greg, would drive past it and imagine a Sold sign out the front. Just a few blocks further along, there was a vacant block of land that had been sold by the same real estate agent who was selling our property, so it was very easy for Greg to visualise that Sold sign in front of our property.

One morning as Greg drove past our property, he saw a Sold sign in front of the For Sale sign. He spun around in surprise and found that for some unknown reason, the people who owned the vacant block had put their sign in front of our property.

So Greg had visualised and manifested a Sold sign in the front of our property, but now he says that he should stop visualising a Sold sign and start visualising the actual house sold.

—Judi Mason

Worrying Doesn't Help

The company I work for had decided to shout some of the staff to a Tony Robbins event, Unleash the Power Within. I had been put in charge of organising this, including arranging the interstate travel and accommodations.

As some of the staff don't often have the opportunity to travel, I wanted to make sure the experience was a pleasurable and memorable one for them. I booked a good hotel across the road from the venue and organised a limousine car service to transport everybody from the airport.

The one thing I was worried about was whether our luggage would fit in the limousine. This was playing on my mind, and I had been contemplating getting another car just for the luggage.

I need not have worried, though, as when we arrived in Sydney, the driver was there to greet us, and everybody had collected their luggage except me. After about fifteen minutes of talking to the people at the service desk, I was informed that my luggage had taken a holiday to Brisbane.

—Judi Mason

Part 4

Children's Stories

"Imagination is greater than knowledge."
—*Albert Einstein*

*"Your children are genius creators who have
just arrived from Nonphysical, who are feeling
empowered. And if they would be left to their own
devices, they would not go astray. They would
maintain worthiness; they would maintain their
feeling of Well-Being. They would thrive, unless
it was taught otherwise to them. In other words,
if others don't do something to change their
vibration, they are in a vibration of thriving."*
—*Abraham*

*Excerpted from the workshop in Boca Raton,
Florida, on Saturday, January 15, 2005.*[i]

An Eyewitness Account

A little boy, about ten years old, was standing before a shoe store on the roadway, barefooted, peering through the window, and shivering with cold.

A lady approached the young boy and said, "My, but you're in such deep thought staring in that window."

"I was asking God to give me a pair of shoes," was the boy's reply.

The lady took him by the hand, went into the store, and asked the clerk to get half a dozen pairs of socks for the boy. She then asked if he could give her a basin of water and a towel. He quickly brought them to her. She took the little fellow to the back part of the store and, removing her gloves, knelt down, washed his little feet, and dried them with the towel.

By this time, the clerk had returned with the socks. Placing a pair upon the boy's feet, she purchased him a pair of shoes. She tied up the remaining pairs of socks and gave them to him. She patted him on the head and said, "No doubt, you will be more comfortable now."

As she turned to go, the astonished child caught her by the hand and, looking up into her face with tears in his eyes, asked her, "Are you God's wife"?

—Author Unknown

*"Only a child sees things with perfect
clarity because it hasn't developed all
those filters, which prevent us from seeing
things that we don't expect to see."*
—Douglas Adams, *Dirk Gently's
Holistic Detective Agency*

Out of the Mouths of Babes

When six-year-old Bella's mother told her that her cousins might be coming for a visit, she also added, "but they may not, so I don't want you to get your hopes up."

To which Bella replied, "Well, I am going to think about them all the time because when you think about things, they happen." (And it did; her cousins came to visit, and they all had a wonderful time together.)

—Judi Mason

Random Acts of Kindness

While visiting my beautiful mother (the author of this book), she showed me some kindness cards, which had been made to inspire people to commit random acts of kindness. The idea was to do something nice for someone and leave behind one of these beautiful little cards, and hopefully, they would do something nice for someone else. So one day while getting some lunch, I decided to pay for the elderly man behind me in the takeaway drive-through. Hopefully, I put a smile on his face that day, but what really made me smile was my eight-year-old son, who was with me at the time.

He was so amazed that we were paying for someone else and so excited by the idea.

He started bouncing around in his seat, talking a million miles an hour: "That man doesn't have to pay; he is going to get to the counter, and they will say, 'It's free.' I can't wait to pay for someone too. You know how people have writing on the back of their cars, saying, 'Don't follow me; I'm going fishing.' Well, I am going to have one that says, 'Follow me, and I'll pay.'"

I replied that everyone would want to follow him everywhere.

"Yeah," he said. "I will probably spend all my money, but I will be doing so many nice things that nothing bad will ever happen to me. I could go to one of those jackpot places, and because I am doing nice things, then God will do nice things for me, and I would win. Then I could pay for even more people."

I had tears in my eyes and a giant smile on my face. He knew how the universe worked. So clearly and with such absolute faith. What an inspiring lesson I got that day in exchange for my small act of kindness.

—Rebecca Malcomson

A Speech for School

Did you know that what you think is what you attract? It's true.

Put your hand up if you've ever had a day that keeps on getting worse and worse.

Maybe a day something like this:

You wake up to an annoying loud noise like an alarm clock or a door slamming. You've woken up, frowning. A cold shower. Not happy Jan. No clean clothes. Oh, c'mon. This day sucks! No milk for your cereal. Could anything else go wrong? Your dog's chewed one of your shoes. You stupid dog! Now you're running late; you miss the bus. I think you get my picture. It's not getting any better.

From the moment you woke up, what were your thoughts? What were you focusing on? What were you attracting? I can tell you: None of it was good.

Now, put your hand up if you've ever had a great day where everything went right for you.

Perhaps you were walking down the street, thinking what a beautiful day it was, and you looked down and found five dollars. Cool. What a great start to the day. Then when you went to spend it, there was a special on so your money went further. Excellent. Then you arrived home, and not only has your mum made your favourite lunch, but also there's a letter for you saying that you've just won an award. Yes. Your day just kept on getting better and better.

What were you thinking? What you were attracting that day was great.

Now, just to show you the power of your thoughts, let me tell you a true story. This happened to my mum.

She was at the Los Angeles airport, collecting her baggage, and she needed a lock for one of her bags. Mum went to the airport shop to buy a lock, but unfortunately, they didn't have any. So she went back to the baggage carousel to wait for the next flight with her friends. She was watching the empty carousel going around, thinking about the lock she needed, and all of a sudden, there it was. There was a baggage lock heading straight towards her, and it dropped off the carousel right near her feet. So you see, this proves my mum's a witch. No, not really, but what she wanted, what she was thinking about, was what she attracted.

I want you to think about this.

What you're thinking about is what you're attracting, whether it is bad or good.

This could really help you next time you're having a bad day.

Change your thoughts.

It works for me.

—Georgie Dunn, 12

Shopping

One day, my dad and I were shopping for my mum, and I was thinking how I really wanted money so I could get the latest toy. Dad told me to check out what that thing was over there, so I did, and when I got over there, I was so excited because there was $75 sitting there. So I picked it up and showed it to my dad, and he told me not to lose it. You know what? I ended up getting the toy.

—Kobi McLeod, 12

Hook

My grandad and I were in a shop, and we were looking at the DVDs. I found a movie called *Hook* and said that I really wanted to see it again, and Grandad said that he had it at home so we could watch it when we got back. When we arrived back at Grandad's place, I found out that my cousins had the same idea as I did, and out of hundreds of DVDs, they had chosen *Hook* to watch, so I watched it with them.

—Kobi McLeod, 12

Motorbike

When I was little, I used to pretend that there was a treasure chest at the bottom of my bed, and I would pull it out, and there would be a motorbike, and I would ride it in my dreams. A few years later, I saw the Crusty Demons (a motorbike stunt show), and then on my eighth birthday, I got a motorbike just like the one in my dreams.

—Zach Malcomson, 8

The Best Class

It was the end of the
 school year, and I was just about to finish grade five. There were three grade six classes and one I particularly wanted to be in.

I imagined myself in the class, sitting at my desk, listening to the teacher I wanted instructing us. I also imagined my best friend sitting next to me because I wanted him to be in the same class too. At the end of school, I looked at the paper with the class I was in. It was the one I wanted. I was very happy. I called my friend after school to see what class he was in. It was the same one; I was even happier. Next year is going to be a good one.

—Zach Malcomson, 10

"For my part I know nothing with any certainty, but the sight of the stars makes me dream."
—Vincent Van Gogh

From a Distance

6,104 miles away from my London home lives a young boy, Yuvaraj, in a remote village in India. I first met Yuvaraj three years ago when I volunteered for the charity Sevalaya. Since then I have visited at least once a year.

I have just completed my fourth visit, and whilst there, Yuvaraj celebrated his fourteenth birthday. I knew before I went to India that his birthday was approaching and wanted to buy him a gift which he would enjoy and which was also educational. I went to the store and saw two things he might like and unable to decide between the two gifts, I stood there for some minutes and imagined myself back in the village. Which would he like? Which would he prefer? In the end I took the chosen gift to the cashpoint to be wrapped ready for travel.

On the day of his birthday, armed with my gift and card, I went to his house in the village. His mother called him from where he was sitting and drawing in another room.

We exchanged some words, and before I gave him the gift, I asked him what he was drawing. He showed me his picture of a man sitting on the ground stargazing at the galaxy through a large telescope.

I asked him why he was drawing this particular picture and he answered, "Sister, I like very much," and pointed to the telescope.

At that moment I gave him his gift and he was thrilled to receive a present all the way from London, but that was nothing compared to the look on his face as he opened the gift and he saw what I had bought for him... a telescope.

This was a perfect example of where I was part of somebody else's law of attraction and manifestation.

I felt so honoured and proud to have been a part of it and see the huge smile on his face that day.

-Sue Humphreys

Part 5

Inspired Actions

*"It's not your work to make anything happen.
It's your work to dream it and let it happen.
Law of Attraction will make it happen. In
your joy, you create something, and then you
maintain your vibrational harmony with it, and
the Universe must find a way to bring it about.
That's the promise of Law of Attraction."*

—*Abraham*

*Excerpted from the workshop in Larkspur,
California, on Sunday, August 16, 1998.*[i]

The Difference

I got up early one morning
and rushed right into the day;
I had so much to accomplish
that I didn't have time to pray.

Problems just tumbled about me,
and heavier came each task.
"Why doesn't God help me?" I wondered.
He answered, "You didn't ask."

I wanted to see joy and beauty,
but the day toiled on grey and bleak.
I wondered why God didn't show me;
He said, "But you didn't seek."

I tried to come into God's presence;
I used all my keys at the lock.
God gently and lovingly chided,
"My child, you didn't knock."

I woke up early this morning
and paused before entering the day.
I had so much to accomplish
that I had to take time to pray.

—Grace L. Naessens

Meditation

In all of my studies and teachings with very successful people, one of the things that they all have in common is meditation. They all take time out of their busy lives to do some type of meditation. Mark Victor Hanson freely admits he spends time in meditation, while others like Robert Allen spend time in prayer.

In this busy world in which we live, many of us have what seems like a million thoughts running through our minds at once. There is so much to do that it seems impossible to sit and meditate. But if you take even just ten minutes to still your mind, you will be amazed at how much more can be accomplished through the day, how much calmer you will feel, and how much easier it is to face the difficulties that arise from time to time.

Meditation can be confusing, and some people think that they have to sit on a mountaintop like a Buddhist monk to meditate. Although that might be very pleasant, it is often impractical. Meditation is a lot less complicated than most people think.

Meditation is allowing the chatter in our minds to quiet and allowing relaxation and inspiration in; it is also being in the moment and letting go of what has to be done for the rest of the day and focusing on the present. It can be done by sitting still and focusing on our breathing, and every time the mind starts to wander, just focus again on the breath: breathe in, breathe out, repeat.

But there are many forms of meditation. Walking can be a great form of meditation, as long as you are in the moment as you walk, appreciating the leaves on the trees, noticing the flowers, listening to the birds, just being in the moment.

Art can also be a great form of meditation. You will notice that when you are fully in the moment, time has no meaning; it seems like just a short time, when actually hours have passed.

Fishing, painting, sewing, pottery, gardening, patchwork, scrapbooking, any type of activity that puts you in the moment is a form of meditation. It may not quiet your mind completely because you are immersed in your hobby, but it does stop the endless chatter in the mind; most of these activities engage the right side of the brain, which is the creative and intuitive side.

If we remember a time when we felt truly at peace, this can also put us instantly back in that place of relaxation. For me, that can be recalling when I went snorkelling, or watching the rain, or feeling the gentle breeze on my face. Once I have experienced these feelings, then remembering them brings the peaceful, easy feeling straight back to me.

The more often we do this, the easier it is, and now, if I need to, I can close my eyes just for a few minutes or even a few seconds and get into that place of total relaxation, and it seems like I have had a much longer rest. I open my eyes, feeling refreshed and at peace.

Often, especially as parents, we put the needs of others before our own, but when we are at peace, we can be of much better service to those around us. We are better parents, better friends, better employees, and better bosses, so take the time to look after yourself first, and everything flows on from that.

"When you understand the Laws, then you understand that it is not more difficult to create a castle than it is a button. They are equal. It is not more difficult to create $10 million than $100,000. It is the same application of the same law to two different intentions."

—Abraham[i]

Single-Minded Focus

I'd like to tell you more about Joshua, one of my four children, who have all contributed to this book.

Josh, as you can read in his story, was not a real believer in the law of attraction; however, he is one of the most amazing manifestors I know. Why? He has the ability to really focus on what he wants, even when everyone around him is saying it's not possible. If he wants something, he knows exactly what he wants, and he is very single-minded about it.

When Joshua was younger, he wanted a black Holden ute. He knew what he wanted, the exact make and model, all of the details of what the car would have, right down to the mag wheels and the price he wanted to pay for it. We (his parents) tried to dissuade him and said maybe he should look for something cheaper, but no. We looked all over Brisbane and were told that model, especially in black, was as rare as hen's teeth and there were none around. If we did find one, it would be closer to $30,000 than the $20,000 he was able to afford.

Again, we tried to tell Joshua that he should look for something else, but no, he knew what he wanted, and that was that.

Then one day, we picked up a local newspaper, and in it was a very small ad for the exact car Joshua wanted. However, the asking price was $24,000. Joshua offered $19,000 for it. The seller accepted, and Joshua drove home in his dream car.

I knew about and believed in the law of attraction, but I still doubted. I really think that is the secret and also why some things seem so easy to manifest and other things seem so hard. It's our focus, and some things seem to have less importance and also less resistance, and therefore when we state it and release it, it flows to us. Something that seems impossible has us hoping but at the same time doubting. Wishing but still listening to the sceptical opinions of others.

If we could really just stay in the belief, regardless of outside influences, we could, and in many cases do, create whatever we want.

So to create what you want, you need:

1. To know exactly what you want.
2. To know that you *will* have it; end of story.
3. To trust and release all resistance, doubts, and negative thoughts, even, or especially, from well-meaning friends and family.
4. To receive. Be open to receive with gratitude.

How to Create Vision Boards and Books

This part is a lot of fun, and the more fun you can make it, the more effective it will be.

The idea is to let your mind roam free, without judgement; just get into the childlike place of dreaming and dreaming big. It doesn't matter if it doesn't happen; it's just fun getting into the world of the imagination and the vibration of creating.

Below is one of my favourite quotes:

"Imagination is greater than knowledge."

—Albert Einstein

What You'll Need

- Magazines, new or old, especially related to things that interest you; for example, if you like to travel, use travel brochures.
- Photos you would like to include on your board.
- Sayings or quotes you like. You can print these out to glue on or write them directly on your board. Really, anything that makes you feels good when you look at it.
- Cardboard or a large book.
- Scissors.
- Glue.
- Coloured felt pens.

How to Do It

Just have fun. Start thinking about what you'd like to create in your life. Find and cut out pictures you like, design how you would like your board or book to look, and start pasting. Add any drawings or words you like or any extra pretty things to your board, anything that resonates with you, so that when you look at it, it makes you feel good.

That is the whole point: to feel good.

What Is the Difference between a Vision Board and a Vision Book?

This is a matter of choice. Some people like to hang up their board so they can look at it all the time, whereas others like a book, which can sit on their coffee table or beside their bed so they can open it and read through when they like. Obviously, you can put a lot more in a book and keep adding to it, while with a board, you need to create new ones when you want to add different things. Either way, it will work as long as you feel good about it and try not to judge. Don't look at it and say to yourself that it could never happen, because as you read the many stories in this book, you'll see that anything really is possible.

Many people now are creating online boards and using them as screensavers. I prefer the cutting and pasting, but do whatever works for you. Of course, you can use all three methods if you like. I have.

How Often Should I Create a New Vision Board or Book?

As often as you like. If it makes you feel good, do it.

If I am feeling a bit down, I might create a new vision board or even read through some older ones I've created. The start of a new year is a good time to recreate our goals and wishes. There is no right or wrong; just go with how you feel (again).

Have fun.

Change Your Thoughts and Change Your Results

Thoughts become things.

*"We are what we think. All that we
are arises with our thoughts. With our
thoughts, we make the world."*
—Buddha

*"The more man meditates upon good thoughts,
the better will be his world and the world at large."*
—Confucius

"Your life is what your thoughts make it."
—Marcus Aurelius

*"A person is what he or she thinks
about all day long."*
—Ralph Waldo Emerson

Everything we look at was once just a thought; everything.

Thoughts and beliefs were behind the telephone, electricity, space travel, and computers. How far have we expanded from the caveman days to now? Look at what we have created.

When we think about the amazing creations in this world, why do we find it so hard to believe that we can create what we want in our own lives? Why do we doubt?

We have to get out of our limited thinking patterns and look at what has already been proven beyond imagination.

The definition of madness is when we keep doing the same thing and expect a different result, but this is what so many of us do. We need to stop focusing on the results and start focusing on what we want to see in our lives.

Thoughts create, so if we focus on debt, we create debt. We keep looking at that debt, worrying about that debt, and therefore by thinking about that, we are creating more debt. It becomes a vicious cycle. I know. I have been there, as many of us have, so how do we change that thought pattern? How, when we have creditors calling us? How, when we have no money in our bank accounts to pay them now, and no foreseeable way to pay them in the near future? Can we just sit in the corner and meditate? Can we grab a box of crayons and just draw our way out of debt? Can we laugh and sing our way out of debt? No, not on its own, but all of that may help. Has worrying about the debt helped? Has all the worrying and planning and trying hard to make things happen helped? What then?

I heard a quote the other day that said, "When God is your co-pilot, change seats."

We try so hard to do it all ourselves. Let go and let God. Yes, meditate; yes, go and play and sing; yes, draw; and then take inspired action. Get into a good-feeling place first, and then act on anything that comes to you from that vantage point. Do whatever it takes to get out of the place of *despair* and into the place of *inspiration*.

Recently, I was going through the challenges that I am writing about, and I was finding it very difficult to change my focus. My husband and I were continually manifesting smaller things but really struggling with debt. One of the things we were able to create was a free holiday beach home for a week over Christmas. This allowed us to get away from what we were focusing on every day at home and to really work on what we wanted to create for the New Year ahead. We spent a lot of time relaxing, meditating, making vision books and vision statements, as well as spending time with family and having lots of fun. One of the visions I had was money flowing to me and all around me. It felt great, and in that moment, I was inspired to contact a particular person when I got back home.

Almost as soon as we arrived home, our neighbour raced over with some money for us. We had been trying to sell some furniture, and she wanted to buy it. Not only that, but her friend also wanted to buy some other furniture we had.

I thought, *Wow, this visualisation is working.*

That same week, I was asked to do a reiki workshop for a group of people. I love doing these workshops. Later, I contacted the person I'd been inspired to talk to. That person became our business partner and was able to give us enough cash to pay all our debts. Now I am continuing the visioning and meditating. Previously, I had tried everything I could think of to help our situation, but it wasn't until I let go that I had the answers and inspired action to follow.

"If you want to find the secrets of the universe, think in terms of energy, frequency, and vibration."
—Nikola Tesla

How to Raise Your Vibration
What Does That Mean?

Everything is energy; every tiny particle examined under a microscope is vibrating energy.

Vibration is a state of being

We are all existing on different levels of vibration; we are emitting different levels of energy. We can feel it when we are feeling a bit tired or unwell; we have far less energy than at other times.

Our vibrational energy acts like a magnet and attracts to us things of a similar vibration; therefore, when we are asking for wealth, but vibrating on a lack and limitation vibration, we cannot attract wealth into our lives. Our job is to consciously raise our vibrations to the level of what we are asking for. This can be very difficult when we are looking at our bank accounts and debts. If we are asking for wealth but vibrating in debt, we can only attract more debt in that vibration.

So How Do We Raise Our Vibration?

Do whatever it takes to change your current focus. Go for a walk, put on some nice music, sing a song, paint, ring a friend (not a friend who will wallow in self-pity with you; that won't help. Ring one who will make you laugh). Spend time with young children or pets and get into their vibration: carefree, happy, laughing, playing, and so on. Start appreciating the little things, and everything takes on a new, improved vibration.

Sometimes, when we get ourselves into a negative vibration, it's like we are in a black hole, and it becomes very hard to see the positives. By working on our positivity little by little, we start to see the light, and as it gets brighter, we start to see so much more than we could before. Just bit by bit, start reaching for the next best-feeling place and then the next and then the next. Now we are vibrating much higher and attracting things that match that vibration.

To climb a mountain, you can't get there in a single leap; you climb it one step at a time. It can be the same with your vibration. Little by little, step by step, gradually raise your vibration.

In summary, change your focus, which changes your vibration, which changes your results.

The Art of Appreciation

The best way to get into a higher vibration is through appreciating every day. Appreciating the little things, things that make you smile.

My daughter sits at the dinner table with her husband and three children, and they ask each other, "What was the best part of your day today?" If they have visitors, they are included. Everyone has to contribute, so even if they had a terrible day, they have to remember something good about that day.

It is a great practice to get into. It seems so easy to focus on what went wrong, but when you are always looking for the best part, it changes your focus instantly.

Starting a gratitude journal that you can add to each day is another wonderful habit to get into. Start writing down things that you are grateful for every day; then, if you are feeling a bit down, you can just open up your journal and read what you have previously written, and it reminds you to smile.

They don't have to be big things, although they can be. It can be the sun shining, the person at the store who smiled at you, the food you ate, the clothes you wear, the wind in your face, listening to music or birds singing, a warm bed to sleep in, the unconditional love of your pets, the earth beneath your feet, laughing, loving, giving, receiving, friends, children, family, and so on. I am a grandmother, so I only have to think of my grandchildren, and I am smiling. I love looking at life through their eyes because everything is new and exciting. Children are our greatest teachers.

Stillness

Stillness is where all the answers are.
Stop the chatter of your mind,
and listen ...
to the silence.
Listen ...
to the wind.
Listen ...
to the leaves rustling.
Listen ...
to the waves rolling in.
Listen ...
to your breath.
And hear ...
the wisdom from within.

Biographies for Some Contributors to This Book

Scott Buchanan is the author's brother. He has a bachelor of science degree as well as an associate diploma of aquatic resource management and a diploma of business management. He is also a fellow of the Peter Cullen Water and Environment Trust and has worked in private as well as public sectors, mainly in natural resource management. Scott has been a recreational surfer for over thirty years and still enjoys getting out and mucking around in the water.

Stephen Buchanan, also the author's brother, is the owner of You-nique Health and Fitness. He is an exercise physiologist, with over ten years' experience. Stephen graduated from the University of the Sunshine Coast in 2003, with a degree in sport and exercise science. He then went to UQ for a postgraduate course in clinical exercise science. Prior to going to university, Stephen had been employed in numerous other ventures. He is a qualified fitter and machinist but has also tried a variety of things from store man to landscaping to sales. After a minor injury, Stephen became interested in exercise physiology, and because of this, he finds helping other people on the road to recovery very rewarding.

Website: www.facebook.com/You-nique-Health-Fitness-1626962347593010/

Sandra and Henry Gosling launched COYO Coconut Milk Yoghurt Alternative in Australia in February 2010. Since then, the COYO brand has gone global and is available in the UK, Europe, the United States, New Zealand, and Australia. If you put an idea out to the universe, it is amazing what will come back to you. Website: www.coyo.com.au

Rachael Bermingham is currently one the highest selling self-published authors in Australia. Collectively, she has sold over six million copies of her books around the globe and has written a new title every year for the last ten years. One of her co-written books, *4 Ingredients*, is still the highest selling self-published title of the past decade within Australia.
Email: info@rachaelbermingham.com
Post: PO Box 1171 Mooloolaba, QLD, 4557, Australia
Instagram: instagram.com/rachbermingham
Facebook: www.facebook.com/
RachaelBermingham.LIVE
Twitter: twitter.com/#!/rachbermingham
Website: www.RachaelBermingham.com

Raelene Byrne is an internationally recognised energy healer, retreat facilitator and leader, meditation teacher, educator of self-empowerment through self-knowledge, speaker, writer, shamanic practitioner, advanced liquid crystal practitioner, and earth guardian.

With three decades of remembering, learning, and practising, the one thing that has been a constant in Raelene's life is the power of free will, the expansiveness of stepping into your own unique potential, and the ultimate freedom of being exactly who you are, always, in any moment. Having studied numerous forms of energetic healing, vibrational modalities, and bodywork, Raelene spent years in service and support to many Hay House authors and leaders. She has realised that the teaching from ancient times, that we all have everything we need within us, is indeed true. Stop, listen, and act on your own inner guidance.

Website: Medicine for Your Spirit: www.medicine foryourspirit.com

Phone: 0404 849 723

Jeremy Donovan. When you meet Jeremy Donovan, a man with an open heart meets you. He is willing to share the truth of all that he represents. Jeremy is Australia's most celebrated Aboriginal didgeridoo player. Jeremy's exceptional skill with the didgeridoo and extensive knowledge of his cultural heritage has earned him the recognition of his peers as a master storyteller and performer. Jeremy is also a talented artist with a growing reputation. His art has now been featured in four solo exhibitions. Jeremy's artworks have gained a lot of recognition from the United States, with large private collections in California, Seattle, and Colorado. In 2007, Jeremy had over twenty works displayed in the Paris Casino in Las Vegas. Jeremy's work is dynamic, using modern expression and deep-rooted traditional stories. Jeremy has been described as one of the most collectable young Aboriginal artists of Australia. He often describes his artwork as medicine for his spirit.

He sees his artwork as a gateway to connecting with his ancestors: "Painting is how I meditate."
Website: www.jeremydonovan.com.au

Sandy Forster is a visionary entrepreneur and mentor to more than forty-five thousand women in her community. She created Wildly Wealthy Women as a powerful, fun, and transformative training programme for women wanting to live inspired, empowered, prosperous lives and businesses. She's also the author of the international bestseller *How to Be Wildly Wealthy FAST* and has won multiple awards for her achievements. She loves nothing more than travelling the world and inspiring others to create a life filled with prosperity, fun, and success. Get your free inspiring *Welfare to Millionaire* audio at www.WildlyWealthyWomen.com.

Namaste Faustino first learned about the law of attraction from the Rosicrucians when he was eight years old. His father had signed him up for the weekly lesson books for kids. Initially, Namaste was turned off by what he read. The idea that your thoughts could affect your reality seemed insane. Everything changed, though, when he used the law of attraction technique he'd learned to manifest a little red radio. After manifesting the radio, he continued testing the law of attraction, and his life was never the same. Over the past twenty-nine years, Namaste has documented more than a hundred successful manifestation experiences that include manifesting trips, cash, romantic relationships, a

diamond, front row seats at a concert, and even a millionaire mentor.
Facebook: www.facebook.com/namaste.faustino

Kirsty Greenshields is the author of *Women, Money, and Intimacy: How to Create Real Wealth in Your Life*. She is the co-founder and director of the Centre for Resilient Leadership, which through its training and mentoring programmes teaches people and organisations to embrace and embody growth with ease and grace.
Website: www.centreforresilientleadership.com

Patti Henderson is an artist living on the Sunshine Coast in Queensland, Australia. She specialises in realistic portraiture, fantasy imagery, and inspirational art. She is passionate about capturing the inner spirit of her portrait subjects, both human and animal, and inspiring souls with her fantasy and inspirational art modes.
Email: patti@pattihendersonvisualart.com
Website: www.pattihendersonvisualart.com

Dymphna Boholt is one of Australia's leading property specialists, educating on success, money, and generating and maintaining wealth. Dymphna has trained and helped thousands of students over the years to reach their financial goals. Join Dymphna in your journey to reaching your full potential and achieving your peg in the sand, whatever that may be, or visit I Love Real Estate for weekly updates on current affairs, economic data, and investing tips and strategies to help you become a successful,

motivated, and amazingly wealthy investor. Allow Dymphna to help you achieve that which makes your heart sing and that which makes your life more abundant and more successful.
Email: admin@dymphnaboholt.com
Website: www.dymphnaboholt.com, iloverealestate.tv

Linda Smith Harvey
Linda is passionate about empowering people to effectively manage their money, teaching them to take back their power around money, get out of debt, increase their income flow, and to get their money working for them.

Linda's success in financial coaching has led to financial planning workshops and presentations, both public and for corporate staff empowerment. Out of this work, Linda created Linda's Abundance Diary in 2007, and this latest 2017 issue was the eleventh edition. Linda's latest offering is an online webinar training, known as Linda's Money School: Abundance Flows.
Website: www.lindasabundance.com
Facebook: www.facebook.com/groups/9265451

Natalie McIvor from Jewel Events is a past owner and creator of Enlightened Goddesses Business Network. She works with women who want more from life and are committed to creating the change within to live happier, healthier lives. She draws on over fourteen years of experience in small business, coaching, and alternative healing arts and is passionate about supporting women to facilitate the change they desire using a medley of modalities, tips, and tools to create lasting change in all areas of their lives. She supports women to feel empowered and enlightened by teaching them how to look within to find their hidden jewels, the magic that makes them who they are. Natalie shows women how to create a life making conscious choices and start living a life they love.

She is an event manager and facilitator, public speaker, body consciousness facilitator, life coach and business mentor, reiki master, author, DoTerra and TriVita consultant

Email: natalie@jewelevents.com.au

Website: www.jewelevents.com.au

Phone: 0402462804

Izabella Siodmak is author of eight powerful, interactive books to support your full connection with who you really are. She is also the founder of Natural Attitudes emPower retreat and the emPower method, which both provide a direct experience of deliberately accessing your love, joy, and passion as well as feeling the power of the law of attraction, through the unique and profound format of one-guest-only mental and emotional wellness retreats and personal conscious creation retreats. Connect with her through her live events and workshops, webinars, or sessions with herself or her emPower coaches.

Website: www.izabellasiodmak.com, www.natural attitudes.com

Sue Moore is passionate about helping women live a healthier life through eating nutritious food and exercising their bodies through running and their minds through believing anything is possible.

Sue is a fitness and health coach, speaker, author, and founder of Run Sue Run. She recently published a book on Amazon, *Just Another 5km*, where she describes her running training, her journey back to health, and completing a marathon. With her coaching, running experience, and eating healthy nutritious food, she now inspires, educates, and empowers women around the world to know that it is possible to heal yourself from the inside out.

Website: www.runsurun.com

Amazon book: www.amazon.com/Just-Another-5km-Tribulations-Marathon-ebook

Denielle Rooney is a personal travel manager. She says, "My purpose is to get to know you better, find out what your travel style is, and deliver you an amazing holiday experience that is tailored to you."

Travel is Denielle's passion; she has travelled extensively throughout Australia and the world. She left the traditional travel agency world to spend more time at home with her beautiful girls and also to give her clients a more personalised experience. Working with friends and referrals only means Denielle has more time to tailor holidays to personally suit each individual client.

Denielle's reputation has grown, and she is known for her amazing personalised service, her commitment to every detail of her clients' travel, and the fact that she does it all with a smile and a friendly disposition.

Email: denielle.rooney@travelmanagers.com.au
Website: travelmanagers.com.au/deniellerooney
Facebook: www.facebook.com/deniellerooney
personaltravelmanager

Christine McLeod is an interior designer and stylist. She started in the industry in her early twenties, when she was buying and selling properties. Every property Christine sold or had valued was styled and presented in a refined condition, with tremendous results every time.

Christine has just recently been named as a finalist in the prestigious Design Institute of Australia (DIA) awards and Housing Industry Association (HIA) awards for design and decoration.

Christine's expertise is mainly in residential but also includes commercial. Christine has worked for and with many clients, including barristers, architects, and many well-known real estate agents, including celebrity agent, John McGrath.

Christine is a savvy designer who does not shy away from hard work and will definitely go the extra mile to ensure her clients are nothing but enchanted with the results.

Email: christine@blackwireinteriors.com.au
Website: www.blackwireinteriors.com.au
Facebook: www.facebook.com/BlackWireInteriors/
Phone: 0422 865 616

Adam Marini is owner of Baylec Electrical and has now built an offshore business, Streamline Group Services, which has a strong philanthropic thread, with a training academy which helps provide opportunities to university graduates who do not have the resources to further their career.
Marini Group Pty Ltd.
Websites: www.baylec.com.au,
www.streamlinegroupservices.com,
www.cleanerleaneryou.com.au

Sue Humphreys lives in London, UK, and works in cyber security. She has always had a strong connection to the esoteric and the unknown. Sue regularly manifests her desires and has created a technique called 'The Prescription'. One of Sue's great loves is to visit India where she is the UK trustee for charity Sevalaya, which helps to improve the lives of some of the poorest and most destitute people in India.
Email: mshumphreys@gmail.com
Sevalaya- www.sevalaya.org

Notes
(Endnotes)

1 Abraham-Hicks, © by Jerry & Esther Hicks
www.AbrahamHicks.com
(830) 755-2299

2 *Money and the Law of Attraction: Learning to Attract Health, Wealth, and Happiness*
By Jerry Hicks and Esther Hicks
The Teachings of Abraham
www.AbrahamHicks.com
(830) 755-2299
Hay House, 2008.

3 *The Nature of Personal Reality: Specific, Practical Techniques for Solving Everyday Problems and Enriching the Life You Know*
By Jane Roberts
Amber-Allen Publishing, New World Library; Reprint edition, 1994.

4 *Creative Visualization: Use the Power of Your Imagination to Create What You Want in Your Life*
By Shakti Gawain
New World Library, 1995.

About the Author

For author Judi Mason, life is an adventure. An explorer of life's mysteries and magic, she's travelled throughout the world and studied with many great teachers learning about and understanding the principles of the Law of Attraction.

As well as having been previously published in compilation books Judi is also a Reiki Master, Angel Intuitive, Hairdresser, Property Investor, Story Teller, Teacher and Student of Life.

Mason and her husband, Greg, have four children and seven grandchildren. Judi currently lives in Queensland, Australia.

Printed in the United States
By Bookmasters